gather & give

SHARING GOD'S HEART
THROUGH EVERYDAY HOSPITALITY

AMY HANNON

W PUBLISHING GROUP

AN IMPRINT OF THOMAS NELSON

Published in Nashville, Tennessee, by W Publishing, an imprint of Thomas Nelson.

The author is represented by Dupree Miller.

Thomas Nelson titles may be purchased in bulk for educational, business, fundraising, or sales promotional use. For information, please email SpecialMarkets@ThomasNelson.com.

Italics added to Scripture quotations are the author's emphasis.

Some names and identifying details have been changed in this book to protect the privacy of the individuals involved.

ISBN 978-0-7852-9269-2 (hardcover)
ISBN 978-0-7852-9270-8 (softcover)
ISBN 978-0-7852-9271-5 (eBook)
ISBN 978-0-7852-9272-2 (audio)

Library of Congress Control Number: 2022930658

Printed in the United States of America
24 25 26 27 28 LBC 5 4 3 2 1

dedication

♥

This book is dedicated to Sam. There's no one else I'd rather serve people and Jesus with than you.

contents

CONTENTS

introduction: the eternal significance of everyday hospitality

*I*f you know even the littlest about me, then the level of biblical hospitality rah-rah in the pages of this book should come as no surprise. I'm a kitchen store owner, a cookbook author, a preacher's wife of twenty-eight years. And I've been feeding people in my home since the day I moved out of the Tri Delta house at the University of Arkansas into an apartment with my husband in 1994. At the church where we serve, our small groups meet in homes. So I went from having a hired cook serving me three meals a day in the formal dining room of my sorority house to making spaghetti, chili, and tacos for my young hubby and our friends.

I was apparently a ground beef aficionado.

We ate prepackaged, mediocre meals with white plastic cutlery from the big-box store while we connected, built community, and talked about God. Over a shared meal, we studied the Bible, prayed for one another, laughed, and leaned in. We poured out grace, encouragement, hope, forgiveness, mercy, and truth while we held Styrofoam bowls of taco soup on furnished-apartment couches. We were fed. We were nourished. We were satisfied on all accounts deep and wide. And the wonder of simple biblical hospitality captured my heart.

Invitations with intention. Welcomes with purpose. Meals that served people and Jesus at the same time. This is why I've been feeding people ever since.

In her cookbook *My Kitchen Year*, Ruth Reichl shared, "When you cook for people, they feel cared for."[1] I remember my grandmother Euna Mae Nelson living this way for as far back as my memories go. She beautifully modeled hospitality and Jesus for me. I would often walk up the winding gravelly hill to her house and find her standing in her kitchen, wearing a half-apron around her waist that she had sewn. She seemed to always be stirring something to share with her family, her neighbors, or her friends who would gather to quilt, pray, or play cards. She made food for those who were hurting or in need. She offered to cook for weddings, showers, and various ministries in the church. With homemade treats in hand, she made thoughtful rounds to visit the elderly, the church shut-ins, and those who may well have felt forgotten. And because she knew that people who are cooked for feel cared for, she would have our favorites prepared when we'd walk into her home.

I spent hours in the kitchen with my grandmother when I was young, seated on a wooden stool that I pulled right up next to her beside her stove. I'd ask questions, and she'd answer. She taught me about food and talked to me about faith. We discussed Chic jeans, Gunne Sax dresses, and which Charlie's Angel I wanted to be. It was during those times in the kitchen with Euna Mae that I learned how to make homemade macaroni and cheese, buttermilk cornbread, and the perfect fried egg over easy. It was also in her kitchen where I learned that cornbread and buttermilk was an entirely acceptable after-dinner treat. She taught me how to properly mash potatoes, how to baste cinnamon apples, and how there was no one else but Jesus.

I never missed the opportunity to position myself beside her when she made fried peach pies. I'd watch her melt mounds of Crisco shortening in her cast-iron skillet, then she'd fry-flip-drain the pies on brown paper bags right in front of me. The smell of sweet filling mixed with hot Crisco shortening on greasy grocery bags was a near-holy experience not only back then but also each time I make her fried pies to this day. She always said those pies were a labor of love. And if you've ever made homemade fried pies, you would surely agree. I remember watching my grandmother wrap individual fried pies in foil and ship them in a shoebox to her son during a particularly hard season for him, delivering a little home and a lot of hope. People who are cooked for feel cared for, y'all.

At the time I didn't think a thing about it, standing so close to her that we bumped elbows while we stirred. But as I got older with a kitchen of my own and reflected on those days in the kitchen with Euna Mae, I realized why she never shooed me away. She was *intentional kitchening*. She knew that food was a means to an end, and the *end* was sharing the heart of God in the lives of others.

In 2014, I opened a kitchen boutique inspired by and named after my grandmother Euna Mae. And I'll be honest, no one was more surprised by that than I was! I never would have dreamed that a retail store was part of God's plan to use me in the hospitality arena. Listen, I was forty-one years old and had never even worked outside of my home. But I found myself following the Lord by opening a little kitchen store with a big heart and bigger mission—to prepare hearts and homes for demonstrating the hospitality of the Bible. I wanted nothing more than to encourage and equip others to embrace a lifestyle of welcome, to recognize the impact of an invitation, and to understand the ministry of a shared meal. To gather their friends and neighbors in God-glorifying fellowship around their tables. To give of their time and resources, their homes and their lives, and their very best baked dishes to be Jesus to the world.

A cookbook quickly followed, filled with approachable recipes and more hospitality hoopla. Then I hit the road, speaking my hospitality heart to auditoriums of women and gatherings of folks around the country and beyond.

This hospitality message is resonating, and people are responding. Why? They are understanding the eternal significance of everyday hospitality. They are finding freedom in knowing that the hospitality of the Bible is intentional and uncomplicated, not elaborate event-driven hullabaloo. They are catching the vision for how their lives, their homes, their tables, and their welcomes are some of the most natural ministry tools God can use to share His love, grace, and hope with the world. They are experiencing for themselves the fullness of joy that comes with following the Lord in His hospitality command.

How we live everyday biblical hospitality is what we'll explore together here. In this book, we'll do a hard reset right off the bat in part 1, clarifying the focus and functions of true biblical hospitality versus social myths that have convinced us to clamor about in a frenzy. In part 2, we'll break down 1 Peter 4:8–11 to see how our hospitality motivation, invitation, and operation demonstrate the heart of God for His people. In part 3, we'll find wonder in Jesus' ministry at the table and the life change that occurred when people encountered Christ in homes or over a shared meal. I've also included a hospitality handbook with all kinds of helpful suggestions for gathering and giving, along with truly inspiring stories of people whose lives have been transformed by simple biblical hospitality. While this book certainly includes practical hospitality tips, it's less of a *how*-to and more of a *why*-to guide. In these pages, you will come to understand what *intentional kitchening* really means.

My hope is that this little book with a big mission will make its way to couches, coffee shops, and tables on porches. That it will be tucked in purses, diaper bags, briefcases, and consoles. That it will be pored over in personal devotional time with the Lord, studied in groups of friends, and read together in ministries far and wide. At the end of each chapter, there are questions that serve as food for thought as well as easy-to-follow recipes, both of which may inspire you to gather and give as the Lord so moves.

Think about this with me: Now more than ever, people are hungry to gather and thirsty for connection. They are lonely and isolated. They are desperate for truth and grace. They are aching for authenticity and humility. They are longing to be seen, known, heard, and understood. They are searching for something to satisfy the void that leaves a purposeless pit in their stomachs. They are crying out for God.

The world is primed for a hospitality revival. And if you have a kitchen in your home and the love of Jesus in your heart, then you are called to do something about it.

My prayer is that this book will inspire you to embrace a lifestyle of everyday hospitality that demonstrates God's heart to the world. I pray that you will be stirred to gather and give. People who are cooked for feel cared for, after all.

PART ONE

understanding

hospitality

CHAPTER 1

the practice and purpose

*O*ver the years, I have probably cooked for ten thousand people from my kitchen. My husband, Sam, and I have hosted kids, teenagers, and college students. We've welcomed small groups, families, couples, neighbors, and missionaries. We've made dinner for folks we've known for what seems like a hundred years and new folks who have come across our relational path. We've cut cake to celebrate a marriage of forty years, and we've wept tears over a marriage that won't see ten. We've gathered people who are like-minded and those who are not. People who look like us and those who don't. The lost and lonely. The whole and healthy. The wandering and weary. The courageous and kind. And big, Southern storytellers who make us laugh until we cry. For the hopeful and the heartbroken, we've set a table and opened our doors.

We have prayed, cried, carried on, encouraged, asked hard questions, studied God's Word, and pointed people to Jesus. In our home, we have gathered formally and in sock feet. We've set a table with pretty plates and linen napkins, and we've lined up foil pans for serve yourself. I've piled homemade buttermilk biscuits in antique wooden bowls that were passed around the table like the finest New South eatery. And I've handed premade freezer biscuits to guests right off the metal tray they were baked on.

And God has changed lives.

Sometimes God has changed lives over plates of roasted meat, with grocery store tulips in ironstone pitchers and full flatware place settings. Sometimes over from-scratch chicken pot pie and Dutch oven applesauce in stoneware bowls with silver-plated spoons. But more often, God has changed lives over quesadillas on paper plates or microwave popcorn right out of the greasy bag. Sweet tea on porches. K-cup coffee on couches. Reheated stew with day-old bread. Thai food takeout in sweaty Styrofoam containers. Craggily squares of Betty Crocker brownies on paper napkins in laps.

Now I know what you may be thinking. Over the years, I've had hundreds of hospitality conversations with folks about this very subject matter. And I know how y'all do.

Yes, I'm a kitchen store owner and a cookbook author, so I feel sure y'all have conjured up a bunch of easier-for-you-than-me excuses. So it's important at this point for me to throw cold water on all of your misconceptions.

God has *not* used our home to change lives for *any* of the following reasons:

- ♥ Because we're holier than you.
- ♥ Because we cook better than you.
- ♥ Because our house is laid out better than your house for hosting company.
- ♥ Because we have plenty of parking or places to sit.
- ♥ Because we're "people" people.

- ♥ Because Sam is a full-time pastor.
- ♥ Because we must know what to say.
- ♥ Because we're in a different season of life, a different socioeconomic demographic, or because we live in the South, where hospitality comes with the territory.

No, God has changed lives because we've opened our home, invited people in, and asked Him to.

I'll reheat my coffee while you read that again. *God has changed lives because we've opened our home, invited people in, and asked Him to.*

You see, as believers in Jesus, we each have a calling on our lives to tell our faith stories, to "shine among them" like beacons of light to the world, as we "hold firmly to the word of life" (Philippians 2:15– 16). We are called to show compassion, to promote peace, and to speak grace. We are encouraged to lean in, to hear people, to see people, to invest in relationships, and to build community with those around us. We are created to have fellowship with one another. We are commanded to love people well. We are exhorted to live lives that exemplify Christ's love and sacrifice for His beloved humanity. And in Romans 12:13, Paul told us one way we can do that: "Practice hospitality."

So that's what we do.

And this is what He does . . .

Fueled by His desire to make Himself known to the hearts of humanity, God takes our obedience, our yearning to be used by Him, and our longing to be joy in the world, and He turns our simple soup things into significant spiritual things. Did you catch that? Simple things become significant things. Soup things become spiritual things. We surrender our lives, we understand the significant impact of simple hospitality, we invite people in and ask God to move, and we set up the alley-oop for God to slam-dunk life change, to show off His heart of service and grace, and to be the one who receives applause. (For the record, the King of kings is the only one I would ever allow to play basketball inside my house.)

When we as God's people seek to use our homes and our holy welcomes to usher in the goodness of God and minister to those around us, the wonder of biblical hospitality takes place. We offer up whatever gifts, whatever home, whatever means God has given us to show the world the love of Jesus and the hope we've found in Him. We invite folks in, and we invest in them. We choose people over perfection. We brew unremarkable pots of coffee and serve Bundt cakes that are better on taste than technique. And we let loose the Spirit of God to do whatever He purposes in the lives of those in our chairs, at our tables, and on our porches.

Some life change we may see; some we may not. Some may be direction-altering, world-rocking mega stuff. And some may be sweet, quiet heart-whispers between a soul and its Maker. Some life change may be immediate, happening right before our eyes in the ones across the room. Some life change may be delayed, after the Lord allows our eternal hospitality intentions to marinate over time in the hearts of those we served at our tables. What God does with our willful welcome may bring about peace and comfort, conviction and repentance, joy and delight! But no matter what, we know this: any movement of the God of the universe in the lives of people—big or small, seen or unseen, immediate or delayed—matters.

God takes small things and makes them significant things. He turns soup things into spiritual things. All we have to do is open our homes, invite people in, and ask Him to.

♥ ♥ ♥

Why do I open my home, invite people in, and ask God to use my hospitality to impact lives? Because I believe a simple invitation for connection and community sets an authentic scene for emotional, relational, and spiritual transactions to take place. Because I consider it holy work to prepare and serve a meal to others out of a humble desire to minister to whatever needs they might have—to be the hands and feet of Jesus, to showcase the heart of God.

I also believe it because, in the Bible, we see Jesus satisfy more than hunger when He got people around a table or met them in their homes. Christ modeled the power of purposeful invitations. He demonstrated the practice of hospitality and showcased all kinds of heart-work and healing when He gathered around a meal.

In Romans 12:9–13, the apostle Paul, who was one of the most influential leaders in the early Christian church, piled on encouragement after encouragement for how we as believers in Jesus Christ should live. It's a blueprint for love in action—how we love the Lord and how we love His people in return. And he gave a clear hospitality command in the last verse in this passage. It's important to note that verses 9–12 address the position of our hearts before God and others: emotions, feelings, values, and attitudes. But it's the final verse in this passage, verse 13, where Paul gave us practical encouragement to act on. Let's take a look:

> Love must be sincere. Hate what is evil; cling to what is good. Be devoted to one another in love. Honor one another above yourselves. Never be lacking in zeal, but keep your spiritual fervor, serving the Lord. Be joyful in hope, patient in affliction, faithful in prayer. Share with the Lord's people who are in need. *Practice hospitality.*

Paul urged believers to share our lives, our resources, and the hope of heaven with the world around us, to display our sincere love of God and devotion to one another! He encouraged us to demonstrate our zeal and fervor, our joy and faithfulness, and the hope of Jesus in the lives of others. In what manner did Paul tell us to live out these things? Through the practice of hospitality.

See it clearly: *practice hospitality.*

Then notice what's next in the passage. Do we dare believe that the words that follow Paul's hospitality command are a coincidence? I believe it's intentional that he followed up his call to hospitality with whos, whats, hows, and more in Romans 12:14–21. And I'm here to tell you that he left few whos, whats, or hows unturned:

> Bless those who persecute you; bless and do not curse. Rejoice with those who rejoice; mourn with those who mourn. Live in harmony with one another. Do not be proud, but be willing to associate with people of low position. Do not be conceited.
>
> Do not repay anyone evil for evil. Be careful to do what is right in the eyes of everyone. If it is possible, as far as it depends on you, live at peace with everyone. Do not take revenge, my dear friends, but leave room for God's wrath, for it is written: "It is mine to avenge; I will repay," says the Lord. On the contrary:
>
> > "If your enemy is hungry, feed him;
> > if he is thirsty, give him something to drink.
> > In doing this, you will heap burning coals on his head."
>
> Do not be overcome by evil, but overcome evil with good.

Practice hospitality *to whom?* To your modern-day enemy. To people who have much to rejoice over and to those who are desperate for joy. To those with whom you may not be at peace. To those who are grieving and brokenhearted. To those who may not see things the way you do and to those whose lifestyles don't look like yours.

Practice hospitality *how*? By being humble, extending grace and forgiveness, and choosing to be upright before the Lord and others. By pursuing peace and letting God work out what you think people deserve in His own timing and manner of choosing. And by allowing good to win.

Then leave it to Paul to mention Proverbs 25:21 to bring home his point: "If your enemy is hungry, give him food to eat; if he is thirsty, give him water to drink." Forgiveness, mercy, humility, and kindness extended via the table.

Do we need to take a break? Do you feel like you have been punched in the gut this early into the book? I'll give you a minute to take a few deep breaths in a paper bag. Maybe you need to walk around with your hands clasped around the back of your head like you've just run wind sprints. Because I get it: this is *a lot*. It is.

We love to camp out on Paul's feel-good verses about devotion, love, honor, and joy. Understandably! At first, being commanded by Paul to practice hospitality is all butterflies and delight; we're good with that. We can get on board with Paul and fix cream cheese chicken enchiladas and a bagged salad for people who look like we do, think like we do, worship like we do, and vacation at the same beach that we've visited for decades. They binge on the same Netflix shows we watch, they voted for the same candidate we did, and they eat Chick-fil-A on the regular. Setting a table and welcoming our friends from church, our believing neighbors, or our longtime friends in the faith is a treat! And let me say this: showing hospitality to the saints is not discounted; in fact, it's biblical.

We were made by God to be in community with one another.

We are intended to gather and to share in the joy of salvation with fellow believers. When we open our homes and our lives to other followers of Jesus, our hearts are cheered, nurtured, and strengthened. Hebrews 10:24–25 explains that when we meet together, we are encouraged and spurred on to show love and do good deeds. We build community, cultivate deeper relationships, identify and respond to one another's needs through vulnerable conversations, and more. Fellowship with like-minded people of faith sharpens us, grows us, and makes us more like Christ. And for those of us who have put our faith in Jesus Christ, gathering together here on earth is a preview of what our eternal feast will be like one day in the heavenly realms. What a day that will be! I get a case of holy chill bumps when I think about it!

But showing the kindness of Jesus to those who persecute us, those who are difficult, those who are rebellious or ungrateful, and those who might embarrass us because of their social status or their choices—that's a hospitality challenge that can cause our ears to ring and eyes to tunnel.

Now I am with you in this. I shared earlier that my husband and I have practiced hospitality with people in all realms, all walks of life, and all circumstances in our home over the years. But did you notice that I failed to insert hearts and flowers and smiley-face emojis in the text? Because it's tough. It requires a level of humility and selflessness that is God-sized. Sometimes Sam and I have shared our lives and our home with difficult people, and our hearts have been passionate and emboldened with faith, compassion, and great purpose. But in full transparency, we have also shared our lives and our home with difficult people out of pure obedience accompanied by some Olympic-level eye-rolling, weeping, and gnashing of teeth. Y'all, I'm not proud of that.

But we obey God's command to practice hospitality anyway. We lift up the offering of our invitation, even when it's tarnished with selfishness and hardheartedness, and we ask the God of restoration and redemption to do what He does best . . . change lives. Ours included.

♥ ♥ ♥

Before moving forward, there's an elephant in the room we must address. It's the word *command*. As I've traveled and seen your faces and squeezed your necks around the country, as I've enjoyed conversations with you at Euna Mae's or in the grocery aisle somewhere between the asparagus bundles and the Black Forest ham, I've heard y'all say this: "My aunt Lorraine loves Jesus and has such a gift for hospitality, but it's just not my gift." The thing is, it doesn't have to be. Hospitality is a command. Mic drop.

Now I realize you may not be fully recovered from that gutsy section a few pages back. Don't give up on this book just yet. The Lord has seen fit to put this book in your hands for a reason, dear one. So don't give up on Him just yet either. Remember, my ultimate goal in these pages is to simplify hospitality for you so that *even if you feel like it's not your gift,* you will still come to understand the eternal impact, spiritual opportunity, and significant ministry that can take place when you open your home or share a missional meal with those around you. So stick with me here.

Let's consider our using spiritual gifts versus obeying biblical commands for a minute, shall we? Regarding gifting, 1 Corinthians 12:4–7 says this:

There are different kinds of gifts, but the same Spirit distributes them. There are different kinds of service, but the same Lord.

There are different kinds of working, but in all of them and in everyone it is the same God at work.

Now to each one the manifestation of the Spirit is given for the common good.

There is so much we could unpack and process regarding gifts of the Spirit. But for the sake of keeping things clear and uncomplicated, I want us to land here, okay? What follows is an explanation by Dr. Sam Hannon, congregational leader of Fellowship Bible Church of Northwest Arkansas (and my betrothed). While sitting across the room watching a World War II documentary, he effortlessly and wisely explained the Corinthians passage above in this way, which I think is really good:

> When a person places his or her faith in Christ, the Holy Spirit imparts a spiritual gift or gifts to them. These gifts are either *new manifestations* of grace *or a special empowerment* of the natural skills, passions, or talents that they already possessed. All gifts, whether new or natural, work together for the common good and God's glory.[1]

Now regarding commands, Deuteronomy 11:1 says, "Love the LORD your God and keep his requirements, his decrees, his laws and *his commands* always."

A biblical command is a requirement, a decree, a directive, or a rule that God has given to us. Commands in Scripture come with an expectation that, out of our love for Him, we will obey His authority, regardless of whether it's in our natural ability (spiritual gifting) or not. For example, in Mark 16:15, we are commanded, "Go into all the world and preach the gospel to all creation." I'll confess right now that evangelism is not my spiritual gift. It doesn't come naturally to me. As a matter of fact, I break out in a clammy sweat when I sense that God is moving me to share the message of salvation with someone, even though I believe the gospel with all my heart. But I have a friend who can easily and gracefully share his faith with a coworker or with an Uber driver like it ain't no big thang. He and I are both commanded to evangelize. Sharing the gospel comes naturally to him, but not for me. But that doesn't mean that I shouldn't obey the directive to share my faith.

Luke 18:1 tells us to "always pray and not give up." Colossians 4:2 commands us, "Devote yourselves to prayer." And 1 Thessalonians 5:17 flat-out declares, "Pray continually." I don't pray continually, y'all. I don't. It's not my natural inclination to pray with the fervor Scripture describes. However, I have a dear friend who breathes prayer. She prays in the car. She prays while she cleans. She prays over people at her door, in her home, at the library, in a museum, at the market, or on the street. She prays right smack-dab in the middle of a sentence when she feels like you need to be lifted up to the God Who Hears. My friend's spiritual gift of prayer is truly something special to behold. And yet, the biblical command for me to seek the Lord in prayer doesn't change, let up, or become optional because it's not in my wheelhouse.

Your aunt Lorraine who loves Jesus and has the gift of hospitality? Well, she was likely wired from the get-go in her mother's womb to be hospitable, to converse easily, to be welcoming, and to enjoy serving others. And the Holy Spirit of God, in His sovereign and strategic way, chose to light fire under those talents and passions in order to use her in His glorious plan for Christians to be Jesus in the world. But both you and Lorraine have received the same command: practice hospitality.

This should go without saying if you are a believer in Christ, but it's good for us to be reminded of this truth: When we follow

God out of our comfort zones, relying on Him to sustain us, to give us courage, and to use us when we are weak, then He is strong. He takes our willingness to follow Him in obedience and does extraordinarily beyond what we could ask or imagine. The faithfulness of God has got your back, dear ones. In all things. Hospitality included.

Practice hospitality. This is God's missional and relational requirement via the instruction of Paul for those who follow Him. Whether gathered with believers, the like-minded, or the downright fun. Whether engaging the difficult, the draining, or the burdensome. And yes, whether it's in our wheelhouse or not, we obey the biblical command to practice hospitality, trusting that God works through our welcome in big and small ways for His glory and our good.

And let me shout this to your heart and to your ears right now: whether hospitality is your gifting or something you share out of faithfulness to your calling to be Jesus to the world, *you will be filled and blessed!* I'm telling you, this is the wondrous and mysterious way the Lord works. We share hospitality, we serve others, and we lean into their lives—and somehow we receive an undeniable, holy joy. It's true. It's difficult to reconcile; it doesn't make sense on paper. But it is life-giving work to give our lives away!

So how do we practice hospitality? I asked myself the same question when I was pursuing the stirring God put on my heart to encourage and equip people to embrace everyday hospitality.

It was the fall of 2013, and I found myself in a new season of life with big kids who either drove themselves to and fro or had sports practices after school until dark. I had more time on my hands than ever before. I had always worked, but mostly from home doing design projects. I worked in my sunny home office just off of the foyer with sliding pocket french doors and Sherwin-Williams Sea Salt walls. Sam worked from home a day or two a week when he wasn't in meetings at the church. And this particular Tuesday, he was working in his study in the basement, just beyond the family room. (His office had zero sunshine and was starved for an ounce of delight. It was more like a dungeon of sorts, and I never understood how on earth he found inspiration in that cell. But a master's degree from Dallas Theological Seminary, a doctorate from Gordon-Conwell Theological Seminary, and hundreds of compelling sermons written in that very hole leave me standing corrected and in awe.)

On that Tuesday, I descended the depths to his work chamber, accompanied by the biggest lump in my throat and a weight on my chest that made it seem impossible to breathe. You've likely been there—when you have to hold your breath to keep your tears from soaking your face and the neck of your blouse. The minute you actually exhale, well, that's all there is to it. I'm sure you've experienced the same for some reason or another.

I sat down in his office, and the split-second I opened my mouth, my tears flooded like torrents. I told Sam that I had the most undeniable prompting by God to put something into the world that He planned to use to influence hearts and homes to embrace simple, biblical hospitality.

You see, I had become entirely aware of how folks had gotten away from feeding their families, from opening their doors to friends and neighbors, and from using the comfort of food and the ministry of home to care for one another. It was true in 2013, and it's truer now. Everyone's just so busy. People have become enamored with curating their lives to look like a social media post or something pinworthy. Their eyes are focused on themselves and their own needs, which blurs their vision to see the needs of others. The convenience of curbside pickup and drive-throughs have replaced conversation and community. The crisis of isolation and distance has hindered our ability to love our neighbors well. The result is comparison, complacency, and closed doors. Missed opportunities to show people they're cared for by us and by the God who made them. Missed opportunities for people of faith to lean into others' lives, to comfort, to cheer, to be joy, and to be Jesus. Isn't that a shame? It's a cryin' shame.

Let me tell you, God had my guts in knots over the condition of our collective welcome. He emboldened me to share the beauty and blessing of biblical hospitality so people wouldn't miss one more minute of the abundant life that happens when they make and share food with others.

♥ ♥ ♥

During the season of prayerful watching, listening, and processing as I awaited instruction and direction from the Lord, I searched God's Word for a fresh perspective that made hospitality seem approachable, doable, and uncomplicated. I asked God to give me straightforward words from Scripture that I could craft into a mission statement, a motto, a battle cry.

Then, on March 31, 2014, I read 1 Peter 4:8–11 with new eyes. It may seem melodramatic that I know the date, but at that very moment, I entered this hospitality revelation in a note in my phone, like a modern-day altar to the faithfulness of God. Here's what I read:

> Above all, love each other deeply, because love covers over a multitude of sins. Offer hospitality to one another without grumbling. Each of you should use whatever gift you have received to serve others, as faithful stewards of God's grace in its various

forms. If anyone speaks, they should do so as one who speaks the very words of God. If anyone serves, they should do so with the strength God provides, so that in all things God may be praised through Jesus Christ. To him be the glory and the power for ever and ever. Amen.

But here's what I saw . . . *Love Welcome Serve.*

The Lord satisfied my search by showing me the commands of this passage in correlation with my hospitality hunt! Do you see them? *Love* deeply. *Welcome* gladly ("offer hospitality to one another without grumbling"). *Serve* faithfully. So that in all things God may be praised through Jesus Christ.

Love Welcome Serve. These words have become the mission statement of my home, my retail store, my brand, my heart. It's the title of my cookbook.[2] It's a hashtag on Instagram. I have it printed on mugs and tees, pie dishes and paper goods at my kitchen store. I've even had it piped on sugar cookies in the prettiest script for special events! While all that is fun and maybe a wee bit ridiculous, let me tell you why I all but shout these simple commands from the mountaintops.

Since we are *commanded* to practice hospitality, where do we begin? Where do we start? What does it look like? How do we practice the hospitality of the Bible? According to Peter, we *love*, we *welcome*, and we *serve*.

Do not miss this—it's big, y'all . . . We love, we welcome, and we serve because *He* loved, *He* welcomed, and *He* served us. Do you see it? When we love, welcome, and serve others through the practice of everyday hospitality, we personify the heart of God. We put on full display God's great devotion and delight, His acceptance and embrace, and the offering and sacrifice He made for His beloved humankind.

Mm. Mm. Mm. That is good stuff we are going to keep unpacking spiritually and practically as we go. But before we go any further in our understanding of what simple, everyday biblical hospitality is, it's important to clarify what it is not.

♥ ♥ ♥

Food for Thought

♥ What comes to mind when you think of hospitality? Dinner parties with china and silver? Paper plates and pizza rolls? Why do you think God commanded us to practice hospitality in Romans 12:13? Identify a few eternal purposes that biblical hospitality fulfills.

♥ If the Lord uses biblical hospitality to change lives, can you think of a time when you have personally experienced a life change, big or small, following a hospitality encounter?

♥ Who is someone in your life you would consider good at practicing hospitality? What is it about that person that causes you to think so?

♥ How do you feel about practicing biblical hospitality? When you extend hospitality to others, do you do so primarily out of passion and gifting or out of obligation and obedience? If the latter, what fears or hesitations do you need to take before the Lord?

♥ ♥ ♥

rustic apple galette

SERVES 4

There's rarely a time when a rustic apple galette isn't just right! This recipe is easy and so pretty. Its free-form appearance not only adds charm and appeal but also makes this sweet pastry treat absolutely doable. I keep all the ingredients handy in the event that I want to fill, fold, and bake one in the oven. This recipe will serve four easily, and possibly six. Sometimes I lay out and fill both crusts, doubling the recipe. You can serve this with a scoop of ice cream—vanilla is tried and true, but also think cinnamon or caramel butter pecan!

1 (9-inch) pie crust round from a box of premade refrigerated pie crusts

3 Honeycrisp apples, peeled, cored, and thinly sliced

2 teaspoons fresh lemon juice (about 1 lemon)

1/2 cup sugar

1/4 cup all-purpose flour

1 teaspoon ground cinnamon

1/2 teaspoon nutmeg

1/4 teaspoon salt

Pinch of cloves, optional

1 egg white splashed with 1 teaspoon water

4 tablespoons unsalted butter, diced into bits

1/3 cup apricot or peach preserves

Chopped pecans for garnish

Whipped cream or ice cream for serving alongside

Preheat the oven to 400°F. Unroll one pie crust that has been allowed to sit at room temperature for 15 minutes or until pliable. Place it on a parchment-lined baking sheet.

In a large mixing bowl, toss the sliced apples in lemon juice. In a medium bowl, mix the sugar, flour, cinnamon, nutmeg, salt, and cloves. Stir the dry mix into the apples, and stir to coat the apples well.

Spoon the apple mixture into the middle of the pie crust, leaving about a 2-inch margin around the pie crust edge. Use your fingers to place the apples so that they're all lying flat. Then fold the edges of the crust up and over the outer portion of the apples. (The fold of the crust will be where the apples and margin meet.)

Brush the crust with egg white so it will get beautifully crisp. Dollop the top of the exposed apples with bits of butter. Bake for 30 to 45 minutes until the crust is golden, the filling is bubbly, and the apples are tender. (Bake time will vary.) Remove the pan and slather the hot apples in apricot or peach preserves. Allow to cool at least 10 minutes. Cut into wedges.

CHAPTER 2

people over presentation

$\mathcal{I}$t was Christmas of 1996. Sam and I had been married for two years, we'd had our first baby, and we were celebrating our first holiday season in a new-to-us house. And I don't know what got into me, but the one-two punch of having a new house paired with the expectations of the holidays did a number on me.

I had spent the first two years of my marriage subscribing to every kitchen and home magazine ever published: *Martha Stewart Living, Real Simple, Southern Living, Country Living, Country Home,* and whatever else showed up in my mailbox based on my magazine-buying habits. Back then, there was no Instagram, no Pinterest, and no digital options to throw into the mix. Thank God for His mercies. Because I'm here to tell you that this young bride who was inundated with media about what it looks like to entertain during the holidays in her first home *fell hard.*

This particular Christmas, we were invited to a dinner party with some couple friends from college, dear ones with whom we had history. Believers who cheered my spirit and felt like heaven to my soul. Like most holiday dinner parties, the women divvied up the list of who would bring what dish. And I was assigned dessert.

My first thought was that I had some easy and scrumptious desserts in my growing repertoire, like a shortcut éclair of sorts and a lemon-glazed cake that was Euna Mae's recipe. But oh no! Once my eyes started perusing the glossy pages of endless stacks of magazines, the devil himself convinced me to make an edible bonbon Christmas tree instead.

Oh yes, my edible bonbon tree would be as magnificent as the image that captivated my heart. A Christmas tree–shaped cone coated in chocolate and gold leaf accents, studded with the richest hand-rolled delectables for guests to select and enjoy. It would be presented in all its glory on an antique pewter platter that I did not, in fact, yet own.

A showstopper indeed.

This recipe required not only a trip to the grocery store to buy 873 pounds of melting chocolate, cream cheese, strawberry preserves, powdered sugar, and I don't even remember what else, but also a spin through the craft store, where I was instructed to buy the following:

1 15-inch-tall green Styrofoam cone
1 12-inch round gold-foil cardboard cake base
Imitation gold leaf foil sheets
18-inch Christmas plaid wired ribbon
Floral wire
Toothpicks
Paintbrush

You read that right, folks. A paintbrush. To make a dessert.

What ensued was really one for the record books. I melted chocolate, painted the bottom of that Styrofoam cone with said chocolate, and hurriedly stuck it to the gold cardboard base. (Refrigerate.) I stirred together the filling, scooped balls of filling, hand-rolled balls of filling, and put them on a sheet pan. (Refrigerate.) Then I melted chocolate in a makeshift double boiler, coating three to four chilled balls of filling at a time in the chocolate before returning them to the sheet pan and sprinkling the tops with edible confetti sprinkles. (Repeat with all 375 balls. Refrigerate.) I melted more chocolate and painted it all over the entire green cone that was stuck to the gold cardboard, working swiftly to adhere sheets of imitation gold leaf foil to cover the whole blasted thing. (Refrigerate.) Then I conjured up all my algebra and geometry skills from junior high school to mathematically and strategically space toothpicks in protruding, equal fashion around the foil-covered cone so that I could stick refrigerated chocolate balls with sprinkles on every last toothpick. And finally, I used the skills I had learned from the florist at my wedding the year prior to make a loopy, plaid bow cinched in the center with wire and affixed at the peak like the happiest tree topper there ever was. Hallelujah, amen.

It was beautiful—and I was mad. I was mad at Sam for no reason. I was mad at Martha Stewart. I was mad at magazine editors in general. I was furious with everyone who ever made Styrofoam. And when I took that festive bad boy to the party, I was mad at everyone who plucked and ate a bonbon because they were destroying my hard work.

Can I just say that the edible bonbon Christmas tree of 1996 looked lovely for all of .4267 seconds before the very first toothpick was exposed? After that, it just looked like a child's holly-jolly craft project gone awry. A deconstructed edible bonbon Christmas tree is nothing to shake a stick at, gang.

We have friends who were at the party almost three decades ago who will tell you they still remember how delicious those delicacies were. But can I tell you something awful that may come as no surprise to you? Because I was so consumed with being fancy and trying to impress, because I was aspiring to live the life of the finest social entertainers I'd seen in magazines who craft the most elaborate desserts, I don't remember anything about that night. Not the food, not the twinkle of holiday decor, not the wonder of gathering with our dearest, not one thing sweet or gracious that the Lord did that evening among friends.

Gross.

♥ ♥ ♥

In order to have a right view of what it looks like to practice biblical hospitality, we need to consider what it does *not* look like. Hospitality is not entertaining. *Entertain* is defined in part as "to hold the attention of pleasantly."[1] Do you get a sense of where the focus is? If you are holding someone's attention, then that means their eyes are on you. The very definition of entertaining implies that you are the main event, the center of attention, the star of the show.

Just think about the world of entertainment itself! Entertainers, whether on television, Broadway, or the big screen, pretend to be someone they're not in order to provide amusement, win awards, and gain applause. They are straight-haired, flat-chested brunettes who put on wavy wigs and tape all the things to look like buxom blondes. They grew up in New Jersey but have perfected a British accent. They sit for hours in chairs to be transformed with hair and makeup and prosthetics galore to become the person they believe *you* want to see, with the ultimate goal of not only putting things into the world that are delightful or compelling but also receiving approval, acquiring fame, and wearing a sparkly dress onstage to earn their place in history. (I'm not knocking the entertainment industry. It's just an illustration, folks.)

When we allow these same entertainment concepts to trickle into our hospitality ideals, we tend to put the emphasis on ourselves, our homes, our presentation, our ability to host. And when our eyes are on ourselves and our ears are listening for rousing applause from others, we miss seeing Jesus or hearing the still, small voice of God.

Unlike entertaining, genuine biblical hospitality focuses on how God can use our lives and our homes to bless others. Everyday hospitality seeks to love people the way God loves them. Biblical hospitality uses whatever home, whatever means, and whatever gifts that God has given us to welcome others into our lives. Isn't the simple purity of that such a relief? It is to me!

The practice of hospitality has nothing to do with inviting people over to see your show. The goal isn't for *E! News* to include your performance or your updo in a weekend review. Those who understand biblical hospitality are not seeking to be highlighted on the Best Dressed list or hoping for a magazine feature.

Biblical hospitality is not about you. And it isn't about others' opinions of you.

But we can surely make hospitality about us, can't we? No matter our walk of life, our season, our means, our haves and our have-nots, so often the source of our focus (and our excuses!) is ourselves and what others think about us.

Now, I don't know the lens through which you view hospitality, but listen, gang: The practice of hospitality has nothing to do with your food, your landscaping, your ragged patio chairs, the stains on your carpet, the dog hair, the cat hair, your hair, the dent in your sheetrock, the mail on the counter, the water stain on your ceiling, the stain in your toilet bowl, or anything else you've deemed below par. Alternately, the practice of hospitality has nothing to do with your designer sofa, your imported table, your custom cabinets, your custom drapes, your Carrara marble, your aged wine, your aged steaks, your ageless skin, or anything else you showcase with pride. The hospitality of the Bible is about vision and purpose, compassion and hope, kindness and grace. It's humble, not boastful. It's genuine, not imitation. It's content; it doesn't compare. It seeks to serve God and His people. It's powered by a desire for making Him known. Biblical hospitality recognizes that a simple invitation for connection creates the perfect opportunity to share the good news of the gospel and the abundant life that comes with knowing Christ.

I'm as guilty as anyone. I lived this way for years, confusing biblical hospitality with entertaining (as evidenced by the bonbon debacle). I was entirely consumed with what people thought of me, my house, and my ability to wow them. Desperate for their approval and applause, I worked really hard to make much of *me*, not to make much of Jesus—overthinking everything and praying about nothing. I nearly crumbled under the weight of a self-inflicted pressure that I was supposed to be, do, host, cook, and live a certain way.

I was sideways and miserable, but God in His mercy set me straight. He reminded me of His ultimate purpose for hospitality and my role in joining Him there. He reminded me that the only opinion that mattered was His. He reminded me that the joyous life I've found in a relationship with Christ Jesus is worth sharing. And He helped me to see that hospitality rooted in Christ has little to do with elaborate, event-driven festivity or the impressions of others and has everything to do with simple, daily God-inspired grace poured out in the lives of others.

♥ ♥ ♥

Have you ever lost your focus and taken your eyes off what's most important? I know I have. Why do we clamor around making ourselves crazy? Why do we believe that things have to be just so? Why do we compare our homes and our abilities to others'?

I am convinced that we've gotten sideways in our understanding of what true biblical hospitality is because rather than looking at God's heart for people and the table in Scripture, we've spent half our lives scrolling through our phones and clicking around on our devices. And what we see persuades us to buy into the lie that living a life of hospitality requires having *all the things*.

We see a long farmhouse table crafted from harvested English pine set in a flowering field in the late afternoon sun. Down the center of the table are lush clippings mingled with clusters of taper candles burning in vintage crystal-and-brass candleholders. Each of the twenty chairs is covered with a custom neutral-linen slipcover with ruffles and a monogram. Every place setting displays a timeless collection of vintage dishes with calligraphy place cards in gold ink tied to flatware with fresh rosemary sprigs. There's a hostess. She's young. Her thyroid is still functioning as it should. Her hair is pinned back in a loose, carefree bun. She's barefoot beneath her long, gingham linen dress. In her arms she holds bundles of fresh flowers and beautiful baguettes.

Women, we don't eat at farm tables in fields! We gather in breakfast nooks and around kitchen islands on stools with wobbly legs. We eat on porches in uncomfortable metal chairs and at park tables that require more disinfecting wipes than your console will hold. Those photos in magazines and online are staged, curated, and crafted. They are marketing tools and management decisions produced by teams of creatives.

There are some obvious indicators that tell us that these photos aren't real life. First of all, lit candles don't stay lit outside. Second of all, who hosts a dinner party of that caliber without shoes on? I certainly haven't! And third, if we were to set that scene anywhere in the South on any date outside of January 1 to February 12, there would be flies on the food, mosquitos on her neck, and chiggers working their way toward that gal's undergarment bands.

Listen, it's important that you understand this: there is nothing wrong with pretty candles and flowers in baskets and ruffled linen things. I find delight in beautiful things and lovely scenes. After all, the God of wonder has filled this glorious universe with artistry for us to enjoy and savor so that we will worship Him in response. There's most definitely a time and place for all the bells and whistles and for creating a splendid setting in order to make a special memory or honor treasured guests. And the beauty we create with a right heart can be absolutely God-honoring. But we cannot listen to the lies of the Enemy, because he will convince us—he *has* convinced us—that in order to share our lives and homes with people, in order to practice hospitality, all those things are necessary. And they're just not.

Pastor Jeff Christopherson wrote, "True hospitality is a cultural expression of other-oriented kingdom living. It transcends regional expectations of gourmet performance and focuses its energies on the blessing of honest and sincere relationships. It isn't concerned with projecting an image of manicured lives devoid of stress, mess, and chaos. Instead, biblical hospitality flips the camera lens from a selfie to a wide-angle, pointed outward toward the lives of others, warmly inviting them into ours."[2]

Isn't that so good? Entertaining says, "Look what I have! Look what I can do!" Biblical hospitality flips the focus and says, "What God has given me, I share with you." People who are cooked for feel cared for. It's as simple as that.

You see, Instagram, Pinterest, TikTok, and other media are the modern-day influencers of our hospitality hearts, aren't they? I don't have to tell you, because many of you have likely gone down the Pinterest rabbit hole. Am I right? It begins so innocently on Pinterest when you look up a new soup recipe for having neighbors over this weekend. Then four hours later, you find yourself outside measuring for a patio extension where you'll run electricity to hang twinkle lights over the s'mores buffet. (Siri, remind me to build a firepit by Friday.)

There are certainly some wonderful things that happen via social media. We connect with people who are kindred at heart. We are inspired by fellow believers' walks with the Lord. We are made aware of ways we can pray for friends, ministry partners, and the church. We find recipes for cookies we didn't know we needed. We see squishy babies in watermelon swimsuits and bucket hats. We watch a cat meow along with a slow jam into a microphone. We watch soldiers surprise their children at school assemblies and boys surprise girls with proposals on quilts. All good things.

But these platforms can easily become crafty little tools that the Enemy uses to tell us lies about ourselves, our homes, and how hospitality should look. Friends, we have a choice to make. We can choose to fix our eyes and our hearts on things that speak life and truth to us, *or* we can fill our minds with things that cause us to stumble, to doubt our worth, that weigh us down with comparison, causing us to close our doors.

Matthew 18:8–9 says, "If your hand or your foot causes you to stumble, cut it off and throw it away. . . . And if your eye causes you to stumble, gouge it out and throw it away." These exaggerated statements are used to caution us that we may have to do something drastic like limit our social media time or close our accounts altogether if our participation in them causes us to sin. Or perhaps you need to make a discerning choice to unfollow certain accounts that stir up discontentment, envy, and comparison. I urge you to seek the Lord in this!

On the flipside of cutting off your hand or gouging out your eye, we find great encouragement and remedy in Philippians 4:8, which says, "Finally, brothers and sisters, whatever is true, whatever is noble, whatever is right, whatever is pure, whatever is lovely, whatever is admirable—if anything is excellent or praiseworthy—think about such things."

Dear ones, it's so important that we focus our minds and hearts on ideals that are admirable and on people who look like Christ. That the images we see of life and home are genuine and real. That the tables we seek to imitate are full of grace and welcome. That we learn to recognize true biblical hospitality. That we cultivate our hearts to value sharing over showcasing, connection over perfection, and people over presentation.

This reminds me of two sisters in the Bible. Let's take a look.

♥ ♥ ♥

Luke 10:38–42 shares a story about Jesus being welcomed into a home, about friends being treated as family, and about hospitality shown. But in this passage, we glean a deeper meaning in which the focus of our hospitality is challenged.

As Jesus and his disciples were on their way, he came to a village where a woman named Martha opened her home to him. She had a sister called Mary, who sat at the Lord's feet listening to what he said. But Martha was distracted by all the preparations that had to be made. She came to him and asked, "Lord, don't you care that my sister has left me to do the work by myself? Tell her to help me!" "Martha, Martha," the Lord answered, "you are worried and upset about many things, but few things are needed—or indeed only one. Mary has chosen what is better, and it will not be taken away from her."

Mary and Martha were sisters who lived in a village outside of Jerusalem called Bethany, and they had a brother named Lazarus. We know from other accounts in Scripture that this family was dear to Jesus. They supported Jesus' ministry by using their home to serve Him and the disciples when they needed rest. So when Christ and His disciples were traveling and needed a place to stay, Martha invited them into her home as she was known to do. Immediately we see that Martha was inclined to show hospitality.

But what unfolded during this visit is what happens to so many of us! Even with our most genuine intentions to welcome and serve others, we lose our focus and become frenzied. And it happened to Martha. She invited Jesus and His friends into her home, then she quickly unraveled. There were blankets to spread. There was food to make. There were drinks to pour. There was a fire to build. And while Martha worked to make an inviting, restorative place for her treasured guests, her sister, Mary, was sitting at the feet of Jesus, listening to His words and soaking them in. Mary was captivated by the great Teacher who was surely sharing things of God. She was focused on connecting with Him—so focused that she neglected to offer her sister any assistance. I can hear it now. Martha sighing, being especially heavy-handed as she set the wooden bowl full of fresh bread on the table, muttering under her breath. (Oh come on—you know you've done it.)

Notice the two sisters' different postures before the Lord. Martha was serving the Lord, and Mary was sitting with the Lord. Martha was fixed on the necessary preparations, while Mary was fixed on the Person. Martha was laboring, and Mary was listening. Martha was focused on doing; Mary was focused on being.

Then Martha called out to Jesus and beckoned Him to get Mary to pitch in and help: "Lord, don't you care that my sister has left me to do the work by myself? Tell her to help me!" Didn't He see how much righteous and hospitable work there was to do? Didn't He recognize that she was doing it all alone while Mary just hung out on the couch? I'm sure she never anticipated how He would reply: "Martha, Martha . . . you are worried and upset about many things, but few things are needed—or indeed only one. Mary has chosen what is better, and it will not be taken away from her."

When I was younger, I imagined that Martha was being rebuked by Christ—you know, like when your mom uses your full name to get your attention because *she means it*. But as I've grown older and studied how Christ surely appreciated Martha's heart to serve Him and the demeanor in which He taught a good heart lesson, I have come to believe His voice had a tender, nurturing tone when He repeated her name. Martha asked Jesus to make a value statement about the situation at hand, and when He did, He elevated Mary's choice. He did not correct Martha's actions, only her attitude. Jesus wasn't being ungrateful for the meal, the kindness, or the place to lay His head, but He brought to light that all the preparations had caused Martha to lose focus on what was right in front of her. The moral of the story is not to abandon deeds altogether in pursuit of connection and intimacy alone—not at all! We just need to get them in the right order. Being comes *before* doing.

I find several things so intriguing in this story. I love seeing the humanity of Jesus and how He needed nourishment and rest. I love seeing the dynamic of these two sisters and how differently they responded to Christ when He was in their home. And I find it interesting to consider how this is one of the few instances in Scripture when Jesus was on the receiving end of being served. But I'll be honest, I've always been challenged by the tension in this story. You wanna know why?

Because I can relate to Martha.

I mean, can you imagine having the Lord over for dinner? What kind of pressure is that? Serving bread to the One whose place card reads "Bread of Life"? How would you like to clean your house for Jesus? Listen, if He is fully God and knows our innermost being, then He certainly knows that we shoved things in closets and behind closed doors. He knows we stowed baskets piled with dirty laundry in the back of the Suburban. (I've actually done that!)

Like Martha, I've invited people over with the intention of enjoying their company and using my home and gifts to bless them, but I've lost focus on what's important and gotten bent out of shape with preparations, cooking, and cleaning. My husband, of all people, knows this. He's been on the receiving end of my get-in-here-and-help-me glare. It's certainly easy to get so caught up in serving that it distracts our hearts and makes us lose our focus on what is most important. Haven't we all felt this tension in our own lives? If we devote all our time to our guests, then they won't be hosted or served. Their needs will go unmet! They do need beds and nourishment after all. However, if we spend all our time in the kitchen on preparations, then we miss out on the relational time with the very people we welcomed into our lives!

So while I appreciate Martha's effort and identify with her dilemma, I am intrigued by Mary's heart. Mary understood the opportunity to connect with the Lord, the guest in her home. Sure, there were some things that needed to be done, and I'm not under the impression that Mary was oblivious to them. But what we see in Mary is that *she made a choice.* She chose intimacy with the Lord. And Jesus affirmed that the connections we make, the conversations we have, and the community we share with people, including the Lord, are the things that last.

Friends, let's choose to value connection over perfection, people over presentation, and devotion over deeds. Let's understand that being comes before doing—and that bonbon trees are for the birds.

♥ ♥ ♥

Food for Thought

♥ Consider how biblical hospitality and entertaining are different. How does the focus of each differ? Is this a new understanding for you?

♥ You've likely found yourself in the snares of comparison at some point in your life. Is there a time when your hospitality (or your willingness to show hospitality) was affected by a comparison issue? What was the circumstance? How did it make you feel? Is comparison something you struggle with regularly? Consider its depths and take it to the Lord.

♥ When it comes to hosting guests in your home, in what ways are you like Martha? In what ways are you like Mary? How can we be both Martha and Mary? How do our hands and our hearts work together in order to accomplish the ministry of hospitality to those we welcome into our homes?

♥ ♥ ♥

pretty pizza and arugula pile

SERVES 4–6, DEPENDING ON THE SIZE OF YOUR PIZZA

Y'all, this recipe is so easy that it's nearly embarrassing. But it's beautiful like a fancy restaurant, and its taste rivals the same! The best part is that it takes all of 20 minutes, with 18.374 minutes of that being entirely hands-off. This pretty pizza and arugula pile is one I make when I gather folks at my table for a light meal, lunch, or quick supper. It's my first choice for welcoming my daughter and her friends, the young women I mentor, or anyone who comes over for a bite for whatever reason. You can easily add broiled bread or a marinated tomato-and-mozzarella salad from the grocery's fresh olive bar, both practically effortless as well!

1 good-quality deli-counter or frozen pizza (cheese or pepperoni are my faves)
1 (5-ounce) carton of arugula or baby arugula lettuce
Olive oil
Honey of any kind
Salt and pepper
Wedge of fresh Parmesan cheese

Bake the pizza according to package directions until it's nice and crispy on the bottom and beautifully browning on top. Moving the pizza pan around from top shelf to lower shelf may help do the trick.

Cut into generous pieces, divide among dinner plates, and pile the center of each plate with handfuls of arugula right out of the carton. (I trust the packaging that says it's been washed. Here's hoping!) Then drizzle each plate of arugula-topped pizza with olive oil and honey. Yes, honey.

Sprinkle the top with a little salt and pepper. Then use a vegetable peeler to shave pretty, big pieces of Parmesan right on top! Serve right away with a fork and knife.

PART TWO

demonstrating hospitality

CHAPTER 3

love: the motivation

$\mathcal{I}$n January 2021, Lauren lost both of her parents. During the most shocking and despairing time of her life, she and her husband, Preston, were not only in the process of moving into a new house but she was also five months pregnant with their first child. Out of love and kindness, their faith community showed up big! They cleaned the home they were moving into. They packed, loaded, and unloaded boxes. They kept Lauren and Preston fed while helping them get moved and settled in.

A few months passed, and in June, Lauren and her husband welcomed Walker, their precious baby boy. Once again, the families in their lives who had loved them so well during their move showed up to help. For over a month, friends came to their home armed with homemade meals and endless encouragement. While people were there to visit this little family, they would take turns holding the baby and fixing plates, loving and serving them beautifully in a time that was both bitter and sweet. Lauren ached for her parents, but the love of the ones around her affirmed in her heart that God loved her and had ordained this season in her life.

In an unexpected turn of events, when he was only twelve weeks old, Walker went to be with Jesus. Lauren had gone back to work the day before, following her maternity leave. Can you imagine the hurt and desperation of losing a child only months after saying goodbye to both of your beloved parents? Lauren will tell you that there is no emptiness like losing your baby, that no other hurt compares. But in a time when Lauren and Preston felt like there was no possible way to go on, their people became Jesus to them once more and in the most amazing ways. Lauren shared, "When I tell you that I saw the true picture of Christ's love in them, I am not exaggerating in the slightest." Without question or hesitation, God's people kept their house functioning and in working order. They cooked and they cleaned. They brought over paper towels, deodorant, and other necessities to provide for the most fundamental needs when Lauren and Preston couldn't possibly care for themselves. They gathered together, wept together, prayed together, and held on to one another.

The evening before Lauren and Preston laid their baby boy to rest, a group of moms had the entire extended family over to eat in one of the women's homes. The family didn't have to think about eating because someone else had thought of it for them. They didn't have to clean up before or after the funeral because others made sure it was taken care of. There were no empty chairs to remind them of loss or pain; instead, there was a table with every seat filled. God's grace was poured out in a way that Lauren says she had not experienced before. She reflected on this experience:

> In the weeks following, those ladies never stopped serving us and loving us well. Gathered around a table, meal after meal, we talked

about anger, faith, grief, and the grace of Christ. When nothing else worked, we drank sweet tea on a park bench just to get out of the house. We ate chicken salad on the couch while looking at all of the pictures we had of sweet Walker. They brought spaghetti, my favorite, and shared their testimonies of immeasurable faith. Through our tears, we nibbled on every cake, cookie, and sweet imaginable. It was a time in my life I couldn't even think of eating, but food somehow made it easier. Those shared meals provided us an escape from our grief. Those shared meals gave us the opportunity to thank God for all He had blessed us with, including the ones whose love for Him was poured out on our lives time and time again. I will forever believe in the great blessing it is to give love and to receive love from others, because how God's people loved us painted the perfect picture of Christ.

Do you see the way that people of faith shared God's heart through everyday hospitality? The depths of despair were met by boundless acts of deepest love! We can feel Lauren's heart when she declared how the love of others felt like Jesus to her and her husband. Love demonstrated through hospitality does that. It shines light in darkness. It brings peace to calamity and chaos. It provides hope and healing when the hurt is too much to bear alone. Love demonstrated through hospitality comforts, nourishes, and feeds body and soul. Love demonstrated through hospitality feels like Jesus.

♥ ♥ ♥

In chapter 1, we looked at Paul's blueprint for believers to live lives of love in action. In the simplest way, Paul told us one of the most natural and effective ways to do that: practice hospitality. But what does that look like? How do we do so? Well, that's where 1 Peter 4:8–11 comes in. In these verses, Peter offered practical attitudes and actions that support Paul's ministry strategy of practicing hospitality. And 1 Peter 4:8–11 is the passage we are going to explore in the next few chapters. Here it is for you again:

> Above all, *love each other deeply*, because love covers over a multitude of sins. Offer hospitality to one another without grumbling. Each of you should use whatever gift you have received to serve others, as faithful stewards of God's grace in its various forms. If anyone speaks, they should do so as one who speaks the very words of God. If anyone serves, they should do so with the strength God provides, so that in all things God may be praised through Jesus Christ. To him be the glory and the power for ever and ever. Amen.

Of the three hospitality elements in this passage that we are spending time on (love, welcome, serve), Peter led with a call to love deeply. And with a resounding "above all" nonetheless! Why is love mentioned first? Why is love above all?

In Mark 12:30–31, Jesus answered the question posed to Him regarding which of the commands was greatest: "'Love the Lord your God with all your heart and with all your soul and with all your mind and with all your strength.' The second is this: 'Love your neighbor as yourself.' There is no commandment greater than these." Jesus said it so clearly. Love God. Love people. Love is the greatest command.

Back to our 1 Peter 4 passage. Before Peter encouraged us to welcome others gladly, before he charged us to serve others faithfully, he urged us to love deeply. Why? Because love is foundational. It's what motivates us to build relationships, to see and meet needs, and to share the heart of God with others. In order for us to embrace the ministry and lifestyle of everyday hospitality, we would do well to explore what it means to love God and His people well.

♥ ♥ ♥

When people of faith are called to love deeply, we understand that our love operates in an entirely different manner than the world's manner, which often *looks* like love but in reality can be superficial, shallow, sometimes selfish, and frankly, just playing nice. We have sure mastered the *appearance* of loving others when in fact we're acting out of duty, greed, or gain. But in 1 Corinthians 13:1–3, Paul called that out as empty noise—"A resounding gong" and "a clanging cymbal," to be exact (v. 1). He went on to say, "If I give all I possess to the poor and give over my body to hardship that I may boast, but do not have love, I gain nothing" (v. 3).

Well, that'll make a girl think twice before posting all of her do-gooding on social media for likes and follows. Ouch.

On the contrary, Christian love lives life in the trenches with folks. It's a love that cares for, grieves with, prays for, celebrates with, and leans into the lives of others. Loving deeply, as Peter encouraged, takes extraordinary effort to listen to, encourage, initiate, remember, respond to, and live in long-suffering with those the Lord has put in our lives. It's sincere and devoted love, like Paul described for us in Romans 12. It's bountiful and profound. It's sacrificial and others-centered. Righteous love recognizes the emotional, physical, and spiritual needs of others, responding with hope and kindness, prayer and promise, care and compassion, and yes, even paper towels and deodorant.

Hebrews 13:1 says it all: "Keep on loving one another as brothers and sisters." Who do we love? One another. Translate that to *everyone*, y'all. How do we love them? As though they are family. Think loyalty and affection. When do we love them? With a present-tense, ongoing, happening-right-now kind of love.

The church is commanded to love everyone in a way that is deep and high, far and wide, continually and always. But I'll be the first to confess that it's hard to love everyone in the way Scripture instructs. I don't know if you know this, but people are *hard*. They are. Yes, it's easy to show compassion toward a precious young couple enduring some of the hardest days they'll ever walk. But on the whole, people are hard. Think of your family, coworkers, neighbors, soccer parents, school parents, your own parents.

Hard.

But God's people love people.

God's people know that every human was made in the image of God, the Creator. They understand that each and every human has intrinsic worth, value, esteem, and importance and is worthy of attention, time, resources, service, and even our very lives. In theology, the term for this is *imago Dei*, which is the creation concept that mankind is made in God's image—a reflection of the perfect, glorious, complete, and holy One. God's people hold to the truth of Colossians 1:16, which declares of Jesus, "All things have been created through him and for him." Therefore, dignity is innate. Respect, value, and love are to be displayed to every person regardless of race, gender, color, creed, socioeconomic status, sexual orientation, political affiliation, and whatever else you can fill in. Everyone is valuable and worthy of love.

♥ ♥ ♥

We recently moved into a new-to-us home after having sold the house we raised our babies in for twelve years. It was the right time and a good move for Sam and me during this season of our lives, even though one by one our beloved young adult children have communicated something along the lines of, "Thanks for selling my childhood memories." *Whatever.* As I sorted through kitchenware, bottomless stacks of books, and apparently my kids' childhood memories (eye roll), I did what all red-blooded, middle-aged women do before a move—a monumental purge. I went room by room casting value statements on what to keep, what to sell, what to donate, and what to store between moves. And when it was all said and done, I had narrowed it down to two categories: everyone else's stuff and *my* greatest treasures. My wedding china, my mother's china, bits and pieces of our collective grandmothers' china. Dessert plates I've been collecting for my daughter's future wedding. Quilts handmade by my grandmother Euna Mae and Sam's grandmother Mama Grace. Special cookbooks that were gifts to me over the years or that I had purchased in cities I had visited. A three-foot paper-mache-and-glitter snowman holding a twiggy berry wreath while wearing the cutest top hat you've ever seen, and whose ten-inch, glittery carrot nose I have protected with my life for eighteen years since my best friend from college gave him to me for Christmas.

So as one does, I spent $374,832 on the sturdiest boxes, Styrofoam peanuts, bubble wrap, quality tape, and big fat markers to wrap my treasures. (By the way, big fat markers give me immeasurable joy, y'all.) And I began to wrap. I wrapped my treasures in layers and layers. I stood over my mom, who was so kind to come help wrap my treasures, to make sure she was wrapping them like the treasures they were in my heart. I wrote in big fat marker what was inside, which side was up, how heavy the box was, how exactly to carry the box, where to store the box, and whether to set things on top of the box. I wrote words like *Fragile* and *Heavy* and *Breakable* and *Please Be Careful* surrounded by smiley faces and hearts and other (annoying) things to protect my treasures. And on moving day, I made sure the movers were carefully treasuring my treasures the way I treasured them in my heart.

We filled the moving truck with all the valuable things, and they headed off to the new-to-us house. Then y'all know this moment. After you load the things that matter, you turn around to find an entire load of weird, random things just sitting in empty rooms with dust bunnies you can't believe you lived with. They aren't worthy of wrapping or being careful with, but they have to make the move nonetheless. The plastic trash can in your laundry room, shower curtain rods, 573 used bottles of cleaners, a massive red-and-white cooler from college, three of your daughter's bridesmaid dresses that you tried and failed to sell on Poshmark. (True things, y'all.) Have you been there? Well, I was there. And because those things of less value to me *still* had to get to the new-to-us house, what did I do? I hurled them into the floorboard and back end of the Tahoe without a care in the world before I and my three-foot glittery snowman buckled in the front seats and drove away.

When we love something or someone, we treasure them. We treat them differently when we recognize their value. My snowman rode shotgun while the shower curtain rods got the trunk. Are you picking up what I'm putting down here? Every person who has been given life on this planet was created by God and for God's glory. They are treasures to Him; therefore, they should be treasures to us. They are a reflection of His image; therefore, we should see them as such. We should love them as such.

John 13:35 says, "By this everyone will know that you are my disciples, if you love one another." Did you catch that? Read it again: "By *this* everyone will know that you are my disciples, if you love one another." The mark of your faith is not whether you voted Republican or Democrat in an election. The mark of your faith is not what church you go to or how big your tithe is. The mark of your faith is not associated with your vaccination status. It's not even because you have earned one hundred thousand reward points at Chick-fil-A. (But that *is* God's chicken; we all know that.) Nope! John 13:35 says the mark of our faith is *how well we love people*! And our deep love for others is what motivates us to share God's heart through everyday hospitality.

♥ ♥ ♥

While we're on the subject . . . hang on, folks. Let me drag out my soapbox. Give me a minute. I'm in a new house, so I'm still having trouble finding things.

Oh yes! Here it is!

We have forgotten how to love. Not everyone who claims to know and follow Christ has forgotten how to love, but some have. And sadly, they seem to be very loud. They look no different from the rest of the world. They sure don't look set apart or righteous. These folks aren't behaving as though they've been rescued by grace from their own brokenness, or from their own sin. They don't promote peace or foster unity. The lens through which they view humanity is blurred by opinion, preference, and judgment. Instead of recognizing the imago Dei in each soul, they look down on people or, worse, look away. I know you think you aren't one of them—I like to think I'm not either—but on some level, we've each found ourselves on the wrong side of love during the last few years.

We must remember that the Lord God saw us at our grossest and most desperate, and He loved us still. We must remember that without the unconditional affection and grace of God we would be as sideways in our lives as the ones we've decided aren't worthy of love. We must remember that as Christians, we have an Enemy who wants nothing more than to divide us, whose goal is to thwart the impact of our collective ministry and kingdom purpose.

We live in a culture that is dead set on finding reasons not to love one another. In recent years, our culture has made great strides in identifying reasons to be divisive, reasons to disagree, and reasons to dissolve relationships. There's a mentality of *us versus them*. There's an upside-down idea that if people look different, believe differently, or vote differently, then they are not only unworthy of our love but they are worthy of our wrath. Friends, I'm here to tell you that we need to do a hard and humble reset before the God of truth and grace, justice and mercy.

Last year, I made my first Facebook Marketplace purchase—an antique three-drawer light-oak dresser that I got for one hundred dollars. Each drawer had the most delightful carved flowers and old brass ring-pull handles. I was tickled with my find and couldn't wait to feature it as the nightstand in my guest bedroom!

In true Facebook Marketplace fashion regarding a furniture purchase, I was required to pick it up at the home where it had lived for years. So Sam and I made a date to drive to the neighboring town to load it up before we enjoyed dinner out together. As we backed in toward the garage and approached the front door to ring the bell, we were greeted by several flags proudly displaying the homeowner's ideologies. None of them were ideologies that we believed, held to, or lived by.

When the young husband opened the door, he invited us in. Just inside the door on the original hardwood floors were scattered plastic dinosaurs and pocket-sized race cars that made me remember my boys spending hours playing belly-down on the floor. The afternoon light shined through the mission-style windows onto a wall filled with books, some open on a reading table by the window. They were readers like Sam. In the kitchen, the wife had linen café curtains hanging in the window over a sink filled with last night's dinner plates that had been put off like mine so often are. I saw dish patterns similar to my own, plastic tumblers from the local BBQ restaurant we frequent, and well-worn chairs around a small table reminiscent of Euna Mae's.

The young man was lovely. Kind, warm, and friendly. He helped us load the dresser into my Tahoe and told us he and his wife were looking to buy the same year and model. He told us a little history about the dresser and how they'd used it in different ways over the years. Sam shared our source for buying vehicles, and I encouraged him in his season of life with littles. And we drove off with a new-to-us piece of furniture and conviction in our hearts. Walking up to that house, we saw ideological flags that had predisposed us to think we might not like them, much less really enjoy them. But that didn't turn out to be the case.

Let me ask you: Is there a flag someone might display that would hinder you from loving them? A Confederate flag? A rainbow flag? A Black Lives Matter flag? A Biden, Trump, or Bernie flag? An Alabama Crimson Tide flag? (Don't y'all tire of winning football games? Can't you let the rest of us in on the fun?)

The answer, dear ones, should be no.

You can love someone who makes different life choices than you. You can love someone even though there has been conflict or hurt. You can love someone you don't understand. You can love someone you disagree with. You can love someone who holds different opinions than you. You can love Republicans, Democrats, and people from every other political party. You can love the wealthy and the poor, someone who is hip and someone who needs a hip replacement! You can love someone from your rival team, school, or business. You can love those who are legal citizens, and immigrants too. You can love people of a different race, gender, religion, or sexual orientation. The addicted and afflicted. People with differing opinions on border control, birth control, and mask requirements. You can even love someone who uses the kitty-face filter on Instagram.

Let me clarify that loving people does not equal condoning all their lifestyle choices and beliefs. We simply love them because they bear the image of God. Bianca Juarez Olthoff for Women of Welcome said it best: "Our job is to love others without stopping to imagine whether or not they're worthy."[1]

Dear ones, we do not love people because they're like us, and we don't deem them unworthy of love because they aren't. We love people because we are called to. Let's do better. Amen?

♥ ♥ ♥

What is the source of a love that is *that* deep? A love that sees others and their worth through the eyes of the creator God? A love that goes the extra mile, that seeks to serve, that desires to nurture and protect? A love that scales walls and breaks down barriers, that doesn't consider difference cause for divide? A love so extraordinary that, by observing it, others see God in us?

The source of love so deep is found in knowing Christ Jesus. Not knowing *of* Him or hearing *about* Him, or even running in circles of people who follow Him. Not sitting faithfully in the same seat in the same church pew singing the same songs for years. Listen, sitting in church doesn't make you any more a Christian than sitting in an oven makes you a biscuit. No, a person who is able to demonstrate deep, divine love is one whose life has been transformed by saving faith in the divine one Himself, the Lord Jesus Christ, whose love is limitless and secure. Romans 8:38–39 assures us of this immeasurable and enduring, sure and strong love of God:

For I am convinced that neither death nor life, neither angels nor demons, neither the present nor the future, nor any powers, neither height nor depth, nor anything else in all creation, will be able to separate us from the love of God that is in Christ Jesus our Lord.

How about that? Good stuff, gang.

♥ ♥ ♥

When God's people experience this transforming love in their own lives, then they love His people in return. In the most wondrous way, we are filled by His love that spills out into the lives of those around us. It's genuine, not superficial. It's significant, not shallow. It's servant-hearted, not selfish. It's deep and eternal, not here and gone. We see people the way Christ sees them. We value people the way Christ values them. We care for people the way Christ cares for them.

One of the philosophies of ministry that we believe at Fellowship Bible Church of Northwest Arkansas, where my husband has pastored for nearly thirty years, is that the gospel travels best on the road of relationships. In 1 Thessalonians 2:8, Paul expressed how he and his ministry partners, Silas and Timothy, believed the same: "Because we loved you so much, we were delighted to share with you not only the gospel of God but our lives as well." Paul and his cohorts shared not only the good news of the gospel with those in Thessalonica, but they shared their very lives too. Why? Because their love for the Thessalonians ran deep.

What does that mean for us? As Christians who have experienced the love of God through salvation in Christ Jesus, we should desire to seek out opportunities, like showing hospitality, to share

God's heart with the world so that they, too, can know the wide and long, high and deep love of Christ. First John 4:7–11 encourages us this way:

> Dear friends, let us love one another, for love comes from God. Everyone who loves has been born of God and knows God. Whoever does not love does not know God, because God is love. This is how God showed his love among us: He sent his one and only Son into the world that we might live through him. This is love: not that we loved God, but that he loved us and sent his Son as an atoning sacrifice for our sins. Dear friends, since God so loved us, we also ought to love one another.

God's people love people.

♥ ♥ ♥

Food for Thought

♥ What does it mean to love deeply? How is Christian love different from the way the world loves? Is the mark of your own faith identifiable by the way you show love to others?

♥ The Bible gives us several reasons to love others well. Why are we called to love deeply? How does the understanding of the imago Dei change our love for others?

♥ What is the source of the deep love described in Scripture? What is the connection between our relationship with Christ and our ability to love others?

♥ How can loving others through acts of hospitality make a difference in the world? Why is it important for God's people to love people?

souped-up spaghetti sauce

MAKES ABOUT 8 CUPS OF SAUCE

Spaghetti is entirely everyone-friendly. And with gluten-free pasta options abounding, this recipe has become a go-to for me for gathering and giving! When I'm gathering folks, I make this recipe and elevate it a little with grated Parmesan or dollops of fresh ricotta cheese right out of the plastic tub. I might even garnish with a little basil if I'm feeling fancy. When I'm making this sauce to give, I'll send it in plastic deli containers along with boxes of dried pasta, a wedge of Parmesan, a bagged salad, and a pretty loaf of sourdough bread. An easy Italian dinner for everyday hospitality!

Olive oil

1 medium yellow onion, grated or finely chopped

1 ½ pounds ground beef, 80 percent lean

3 teaspoons jarred minced garlic

2 (24-ounce) jars marinara sauce

2 teaspoons granulated garlic

2 teaspoons brown sugar

2 teaspoons dried oregano or Italian seasoning blend

Pinch of red pepper flakes

2 tablespoons butter

Salt and pepper to taste

In a saucepan drizzled with olive oil over medium heat, sauté the onion until tender, about 3 minutes. Add the ground beef and cook through, stirring and crumbling with a utensil as it cooks. Add minced garlic and stir for one minute, then add the jars of marinara sauce. Stir in granulated garlic, brown sugar, dried oregano or Italian seasoning, and red pepper flakes.

Bring to a simmer, add 2 tablespoons of butter, and stir in salt and pepper to taste. Allow to simmer uncovered over medium-low heat for at least 30 minutes to develop flavors, stirring occasionally.

Taste and adjust seasonings as desired. Serve with a pound of cooked spaghetti noodles, penne, rigatoni, or your favorite pasta.

note

- ♥ This is a meal I keep at the ready in my pantry and fridge. Or I'll spend a Saturday making a double batch and then portioning and freezing it in 32-ounce plastic containers for future gathering and giving.

CHAPTER 4

welcome: the invitation

$\mathcal{I}$n our earliest years of marriage and ministry, there was a family who modeled genuine biblical hospitality for us. As I mentioned earlier, our church operates on the mindset that some of the most significant God-work, some of the most meaningful life change, happens in homes. Jim and Pam believed it too. They opened their home and extended a welcome to everyone from every walk of life. High school boys who smelled like gym socks and Nacho Cheese Doritos. Junior high girls who were big on hair and bigger on emotions. Adults who loved Jesus and others well, and those who couldn't find a way to love themselves. People who had all the means in the world, and those to whom the world had been mean. Black folks, white folks, and everything-in-between folks. The hurting and homeless. The comfortable and rich. From the down-and-out to city officials, they extended a holy welcome.

Jim and Pam both worked. They had three young children who

were very involved in school and church, who required being driven all over the place for cheer, soccer, piano, school plays, school supplies, and school open houses. But in the middle of their busy lives, they ministered to people, led people, and met needs of all kinds. During this particular season of our early ministry life, my husband and I led two small groups that met in Jim and Pam's home. There was a regular leaders' meeting in addition to a 6:30 a.m. ministry breakfast that they hosted as well. Sam and I have laughed that we likely spent as much time at Jim and Pam's house as we did our own.

The parking wasn't ideal with their split-level home on the tippy top of a blind hill. While their home was lovely, it wasn't fancy. Their living room was spacious, but it wasn't well lit, and it wasn't even entirely furnished. What furniture they had didn't come from Pottery Barn, the drapes weren't custom, and the pillows weren't stuffed with organic down. The rooms weren't arranged and the tables weren't styled by a published, up-and-coming designer in the event that *Southern Living* stopped by. Instead, pieces were unconventionally pushed to the outer walls in order to make the most room for the most people for the most impact. The rugs weren't pristine, and the kitchen wasn't huge. But Jim and Pam always beckoned us in.

And although they'd consider themselves better fishermen than cooks, they always had food. Nothing gourmet, but it did the trick: Rotel cheese dip and Rice Krispies Treats. I consider them Pam's signature dishes! We washed them down with store-brand two-liters of soda served in red plastic cups that would be stacked, washed, and put out the next time we were together.

Night after night, week after week, year after year, people would cram into their kitchen, shoulder to shoulder, where Jim and Pam would feed us, sit with us, laugh with us, and pray over us. They would lean in, share their wisdom, tell their stories, and show us Jesus. They opened their home, their lives, and their hearts. They used their home to welcome people with intention and grace. They were passionate about people and the gospel. To this day, there are undoubtedly hundreds who would tell you that their hearts, their faith, and their lives were made richer by being inside the walls of that home on a blind hill.

Now *that's* a welcome.

♥ ♥ ♥

What does it mean to welcome? By definition, *welcome* means to receive something or someone with happiness and pleasure, or to receive with gladness and delight.[1] And God's people who love people know that all guests are desirable and worthy of welcome.

Does a worthy welcome require hosting large groups of teenagers and others in our homes several times a week, like Jim and Pam did? Absolutely not, but it does require our obedience combined with a certain spirit.

Here's what 1 Peter 4:8–11 says about our welcome:

Above all, love each other deeply, because love covers over a multitude of sins. *Offer hospitality to one another without grumbling.* Each of you should use whatever gift you have received to serve others, as faithful stewards of God's grace in its various forms. If anyone speaks, they should do so as one who speaks the very words of God. If anyone serves, they should do so with the strength God provides, so that in all things God may be praised through Jesus Christ. To him be the glory and the power for ever and ever. Amen.

"Offer hospitality to one another without grumbling," Peter said. Scripture tells us two things here. One, we should embrace a lifestyle of hospitality; and two, our welcome should be extended with gladness, joy, and good cheer. *But, Peter, I work a full-time job! But, Peter, I have children who require my attention and never leave me alone! But, Peter, I'm exhausted! But, Peter, I'll do all the work alone because my husband is a lazy, no-good man. But, Peter, I hate the color of my cabinets! But, Peter, what would we talk about? But, Peter, I feel sure that someone else will meet their needs. But, Peter, what if they want to become, like, real friends? But, Peter, I don't even like those people!*

Listen, I'm with you. The reason I could list those grumbles, complaints, and excuses is because I've said them all. To Sam. *About Sam.* To my friend Beth. To the Lord Himself. I'm not proud, but I'm willing to humiliate myself for your spiritual growth. Why did omniscient God in His sovereign way inspire the apostle Peter to address grumbling associated with hospitality? Because He knows that we would be inclined to complain and make excuses. Because He knows that opening our lives and homes to others requires sacrifice. Because He made women, for cryin' out loud. He made us, so He gets us, y'all.

As Briana Stensrud, director of Women of Welcome, wrote, "If Jesus' welcome to us cost his life, why would we think our welcome to others wouldn't cost us the same?"[2]

We see all through Scripture the value and spiritual implications of a life given to hospitality. In fact, it is so important to the Christian faith that living hospitably is listed as a requirement for church leaders in Titus 1:8. Why? Because when we practice hospitality, we are being Jesus to the world.

Not only does our welcome promote kindness and grace, community and goodwill, but it also demonstrates God's heart—His heart that sees, accepts, loves, nourishes, and satisfies. As we saw earlier, our welcome creates opportunities for God to turn soup things into spiritual things. And understanding the spiritual and relational significance of our welcome may, in fact, replace your grumbling with gladness!

♥ ♥ ♥

Welcoming others gives people a place to belong. Look at these synonyms for belonging: *affiliation, acceptance, connection, union, closeness, kinship, partnership,* and *fellowship.* Don't you feel those words all over you? It's because we all yearn for a sense of togetherness, to feel welcomed. And our holy welcome goes both ways! It not only reaches out with joy and initiates with intention, but the fundamental purpose of welcome is also achieved when we gladly receive an invitation to participate in life with others.

You see, we were created by God to live in relationship with one another. God intended for us to do life together! As a matter of fact, the word *together* is used 387 times in the Bible. Even in the very beginning, in the garden of Eden, God saw that Adam was alone and declared that he needed a companion. Genesis 2:18 says, "The LORD God said, 'It is not good for the man to be alone. I will make a helper suitable for him.'" In this particular instance, God was specifically addressing marriage; however, this verse also delivers a timeless and general principle for all people: by God's great design, it's not good for anyone to be alone. And what did God prescribe for the one who was alone? Help.

This idea is described practically and metaphorically by King Solomon in Ecclesiastes 4:9–12:

Two are better than one, because they have a good return for their labor: If either of them falls down, one can help the other up. But pity anyone who falls and has no one to help them up. Also, if two lie down together, they will keep warm. But how can one keep warm alone? Though one may be overpowered, two can defend themselves. A cord of three strands is not quickly broken.

We need one another. We need one another in physical, emotional, and spiritual ways. Solomon affirmed this concept that a friend or companion is good, but to be surrounded by community is even better! Think about a bungee cord, which is made up of multiple strands woven together. Consider the weight it can bear and the security it provides amid the twists, the turns, and the pulling. Bungee cords are so secure that some braver-than-me people even strap themselves in them and jump headfirst off bridges into ravines just for fun. (Is that fun? Really? I'll never know, y'all.) This relational bond is what we desire deep inside. We need others in our lives to strengthen us, encourage us, and show us God. We need others who will come alongside us during life's twists and turns, who will lighten the load, share the burden, and make life fun!

As believers, building intentional community with other people of faith is invaluable. There is countless encouragement in Scripture that expresses the worth of church unity and togetherness, both spiritual togetherness (unity) and physical togetherness (proximity). In the original language, the New Testament word for "fellowship" is *koinonia*, which expresses the idea that being together is mutually beneficial. Hebrews 10:24–25 urges us to fellowship with other believers, saying, "And let us consider how we may spur one another on toward love and good deeds, not giving up meeting together, as some are in the habit of doing, but encouraging one another—and all the more as you see the Day approaching."

When we use our welcome to build relationships with people of faith, we are mutually encouraging one another to love deeply and to do good works. And when believers show a watching world how we love one another, it makes an impression on unbelievers. Remember John 13:35? Jesus said, "By this everyone will know that you are my disciples, if you love one another." Our love for others *and* the way we live in *koinonia* with fellow Christians demonstrates God's heart to the world!

Our extended welcomes and our received invitations within the church make our faith stronger and our impact more effective. Our lives are made to look more like Christ. Our fellowship allows for hurts, needs, and even sin issues to be shared. We strengthen one another with truth and heal one another with grace. Our openness leads to belonging; our belonging empowers us to minister to one another and to the world. And the world sure needs us. It needs to know the heart of God shown to humankind through hope found in Christ Jesus.

To all people, whether believers or unbelievers, a welcome extends an invitation for connection in a disconnected world. I know we have wireless things and FaceTime and Bluetooth and Instagram—all kinds of technologies that are designed to make a big world feel small. But somehow all those efforts to connect us are isolating us all the more. Social media relationships are replacing true, in-person friendships. We spend our time watching how other people live their lives while we're completely disengaged from living *real life* with *real humans*. Social media relationships do not replace, cannot replicate, and will never satisfy our deepest God-given desire for community.

It should come as no surprise that there is a marked increase in despair and mental health issues that stems from our isolation from one another. A global pandemic certainly did not help things, but in 2018, before COVID ever came into existence, Great Britain appointed a Minister of Loneliness, whose job it would be to "tackle the sad reality of modern life."[3] They issued nationwide polls and questionnaires, worked with mental health professionals, and ultimately agreed on massive funding for large initiatives to help alleviate the loneliness crisis among their people. Several of their strategies included pairing people in home-sharing schemes and creating befriending connections in neighborhoods. All that research and effort boiled down to this: building relationships through welcome. Why is welcome an answer for loneliness and despair? Because we were created for connection and community, for fellowship through friendship, and to feel like we belong.

Church, this isn't rocket science! God has put the ball on the tee for us. Do you see it? The world is primed for a hospitality revival! People need to know there is a God who loves them, who is near to them, who created them on purpose for a purpose, and who deems them so valuable that He gave His only Son to ransom their souls. Our extended invitation shows the hurting and lonely, the isolated and despairing, that they are included, remembered, and welcomed. Our invitation extended to fellow believers fortifies faith and friendship, provides accountability and truth, and promotes peace and unity. Others need to know that they are welcome not only in our lives but in the family of God as well. Shauna Niequist shared recently on Instagram, "Now is not the time to be stingy with love & care, not with ourselves, not with each other."[4] Oh, may we live with wide welcomes that lavish care on the world around us!

♥ ♥ ♥

When I was in my late twenties, my friend and mentor Sue invited me to her house for lunch. It was my first time being in her home. I loved seeing her fondness for blue and white and how her kitchen opened out to a tree-canopied deck. I admired the coziness of the library in their home, filled with well-read books and journals. Her style was classic and traditional with nods to the England that she loved. Being inside the walls of her home told me so much more about her heart, her life, and her story. But nothing about that day left a stronger impression on me than when her husband, whom I was unaware had been working from home, walked into the kitchen.

You see, Tom is a well-known businessman and prolific author. He is published globally and is a force in the ministry and corporate worlds. And he walked into the kitchen wearing socks. Socks! Well, he had on clothes with socks. But socks. This distinguished man in countless circles who had immeasurable influence on men, women, businesses, and churches alike wandered into the kitchen wearing socks. Grayish brown, tweedy socks. He became so human. I mean, I wear socks! Sam wears socks! My dad wears socks! But seeing Tom in his home, comfortable and ordinary, made him more than the man whose name is on books and blogs; he became real.

It's one thing to be acquainted with someone, and it's another thing to spend time with them. But it's altogether greater to invite them into your home. You aren't with them in the breakroom making small talk and drinking stale office coffee that tastes like tomato soup. You aren't together at a restaurant fighting to have conversation over a loud playlist. You aren't at a ball field, at a bowling alley, or even in the church foyer. Instead, you're beyond the threshold of your door, inside the walls of your home, where you're the most *you*.

People who come to your home get to see how you live and what you value. They observe how you interact with your teenagers, your spouse, or your roommates. They hear the voice you use when you talk to your pets. They gather at the table where your kids do their homework and where you eat Kraft Macaroni & Cheese. They sip coffee on the couches where you binge Netflix and fold your whites. They see what books are beside your reading chair. Are you a big TV, small TV, or no TV watcher? Are you a floral, musky, or citrus candle burner? Are you a neat freak, a tidy pile-maker, or a clutter lover? Do you own a label maker? And when you welcome others across the threshold of your home, they learn one of *the most* telling things about who you are as a human being: are you a toilet-paper-over-the-top or toilet-paper-under-the-bottom person?

While we're at it, I believe you can tell a lot about a person from the orientation of their toilet paper roll. I unashamedly confess right now that I've been in some of your homes and have unsprung and reoriented your toilet paper rolls on your behalf. I consider it my holy duty so that you will be found righteous before God. And for the record, it *is* officially toilet-paper-over-the-top. How do I know? Because one time when I shared this illustration to a group in Houston, a lady from the US Patent Office who was in the audience told me that it is, in fact, toilet-paper-over-the-top. She then referenced patent number 465,558, filed on December 22, 1891. And all God's rule-followers said, "Amen!"

Where was I? Oh yes! When we extend a welcome, when we invite others beyond the threshold of our homes and into our real lives, it builds trust. That level of welcome says, "I'm willing to open myself up to you. Will you be willing to open yourself to me?"

I believe one of the reasons for the incredible appeal of social media is that we're allowed real-life peeks inside famous people's homes and lives that make them seem more like us than different. Gone is the day of celebrities appearing idol-like, untouchable, aloof, far off. Gone is the day of having to wait until next week's episode of *MTV Cribs*, when we get to peek inside Mariah Carey's refrigerator. Now we are regularly invited in to see Jennifer Garner in a gray T-shirt and jeans attempting to bathe her colossal cat named Moose in the kitchen sink. We are invited into the lives of Thomas Rhett and his wife, Lauren, in everyday clothes, playing in the snow like we do, trying to put together complicated Santa toys at midnight, and snort-laughing at the hilarious things their young girls do. We are invited into Al Roker's life, where we see him prepare healthy meals, drive to church on Sundays to worship, and narrate his morning bike ride to 30 Rock, where he delivers the weather. We appreciate finding common ground when we are welcomed into their lives. We delight that they are, in fact, ordinary.

In their book *The Simplest Way to Change the World*, Dustin Willis and Brandon Clements said, "The world could use more ordinary Christians opening their ordinary lives so others can see what life in light of the gospel looks like. And what better place to watch Christians than in their homes?"[5]

When we extend a welcome by opening our homes and our lives, it speaks volumes because it's intimate and vulnerable and real. *You* become relatable and regular, approachable and accessible. *You* become ordinary in the most extraordinary and holy way.

♥ ♥ ♥

For so many of us, our homes are considered our most honored place, our haven, where our peace is restored, where we experience healing from the distress of the world, where we savor God's grace in our lives. And I pray through the Lord's mercy and goodness that your home serves that purpose in your life as it should! I've heard it shared that our homes are intended to be an anchor, a port in a storm, a refuge, a happy place to dwell, a place where we are loved and where we can love. Our homes should provide security and strength. Our homes are a harbor and shield. They offer an abiding place of delight and joy. And note this: our homes are not only where we receive love but also *where we demonstrate love to others*.

Are you following me here? If our homes are places of solace that God uses to promote healing, where we are able to feel loved and become whole, then imagine the powerful ministry our homes can provide to the ones we welcome. Our homes and our intentional invitations can be life-giving to neighbors, friends, and beyond. To those who have also been battered against the rocks. To those who are seeking genuine friendship. To those who need to breathe or laugh or be known. To those who need to taste the goodness of God. Yes, your home is intended to be your pleasure and peace, but it's also a strategic springboard of opportunity to share your life, the love of Jesus, and the heart of God with the world.

Your home is a mission field, not a museum.

Sit with that for a minute.

Our homes and lives are not intended to be on display, protected by stanchions or glass. We shouldn't value our belongings or possessions so highly that people are discouraged from experiencing community with us. We shouldn't be so set in our ways—the walk-heres, sit-heres, be-quiet-in-heres—that they deter us from opening our doors. Our homes are not exclusively ours or off-limits to guests. No, as followers of Christ, we recognize that our homes were included when we surrendered our all to Him.

Jim and Pam knew that their home was a mission field, not a museum, having given their lives to the ministry of hospitality. Jim was heard saying time and time again, "Our house is the Lord's; He can use it however He wants." Do you hear the welcome? Do you notice the purpose? Can you sense the surrender? Can you say the same?

Many years ago, I traveled to Southern California with my friend Kristi. She was an Arkansas transplant who was returning for a visit to the West Coast to see beloved family. It was in the springtime, when there was a legendary home and garden tour that had taken place for years, and she knew I'd savor the experience of it all. So she invited me to go. At the time, I had three children under the age of eight, so I would've been thrilled even if she'd said we were visiting the Museum of Tires and Lube!

As expected, the home tour did not disappoint. It was a glorious day when we waltzed in and out of some of the most spectacular historical homes. There was magnificent upholstered furniture, fabulous art, and lush layers of linens that made you secretly yearn to run-dive-flop on the beds. There were incredible pools, patios, and porches. And there were some kitchens that I'll never shake from my memory. The trim, the cabinets, the wainscoting. *The windows.*

In one of the homes where we were allowed to use the restroom, I kid you not, I unsprung and reoriented the toilet paper roll. True story.

And while the homes were exquisitely beautiful with immeasurable design and charm, I couldn't help but wonder about the people who lived in them. What were they like? How did they spend their time? Did they have children or grandchildren? Were they people of faith? How did they laugh? Do they iron their sheets? Did they listen to Garth Brooks or Maroon 5? Did they ever eat microwave corn dogs?

And although I thoroughly enjoyed being inside their homes and was grateful for their willingness to allow us to browse, I longed to know the people, to know their ordinary, to know their hearts, to discover our common ground. Their houses may have been open to us, but it's the people inside, the connection they offer, and the lives they live that make it a place of welcome.

Your home is a mission field, not a museum—meant to be life-giving, abounding in grace and welcome for the glory of God.

♥ ♥ ♥

I shared with you much of my hospitality journey earlier in this book, explaining how the Lord has been teaching me to value people over presentation and connection over perfection. He has been opening my eyes to the wonder of welcoming others into my life and home. Notice I said "teaching"—it's certainly an ongoing process for me. This journey has been a long one. I'll be the first to tell you I still have moments of panic, grumbling, a desire to please, and getting things upside-down in order of importance. I can still come up with a host of hesitations and endless excuses for not opening my door. There's me, coming clean again!

But of all the things I have learned in this endeavor, this may be the most eye-opening of all: *biblical hospitality initiates.* Biblical hospitality is more than the warm *idea* of welcome and more than a declared, "We should get together sometime!" Biblical hospitality doesn't sit on its hands and wait to be invited. No, a life given to hospitality moves beyond good intentions to action.

When I was in my twenties, I had a precious Bible study leader named Betty who actively and charitably initiated hospitality moments as a way of life. She would hear of a need and respond with the comfort of food and the ministry of presence. She would sense a relational hunger or spiritual thirst and initiate a hospitality encounter. Once, ringing my doorbell with cough syrup and soup in hand, Betty demonstrated the heart of God to me when my entire household was down for the count. I marveled at her obedience, her abundant generosity, and her availability to sweep in and serve. I sought her wisdom, asking her to share with me her hospitality ways.

Betty encouraged me to tune my ears to hear the needs of others. She described her God-inspired intuition and compassion like a radar sweep. She explained that she asked the Lord to help her live in awareness of others' needs and to direct her heart to make a sweep, sensing who shows up in her sphere of influence that she can serve each day. And that's what a life given to hospitality does. It's wide-eyed and welcoming. It surveys, it senses, and it serves.

Why? Because God's people love people. They have surrendered their all to be used by God to change lives. So they open their homes and their hearts, invite people in, and ask Him to. As Ann Voskamp once said, "Our theology is best expressed in our hospitality. How do we open our hands, our hearts, and our lives and live wide open?"[6]

♥ ♥ ♥

Food for Thought

♥ Have you ever received an invitation to join someone for a meal inside their home, and it meant a lot to you? Why did it impact you and how? How does receiving an invitation make you feel valued?

♥ How does being welcomed into someone's home elevate your intimacy with that person? In your own life, have you either opened your home or received an invitation to someone's home resulting in greater intimacy or a more meaningful relationship?

♥ First Peter 4:9 says to "offer hospitality to one another without grumbling." Have you been guilty of grumbling your way through serving others in your home? If so, how? How can a new understanding of biblical hospitality turn your grumbling into a glad welcome instead?

♥ Why is it important to take initiative in extending welcomes or creating hospitality encounters? How does initiative differ from good intentions?

♥ ♥ ♥

chunky candy bar rice krispies treats

MAKES 9 BIG SQUARES

The original recipe for Rice Krispies Treats is always a hit with folks young and old. An old faithful, for sure! But these chunky candy bar marshmallow treats will make your heart sing. They are show-stopping, chewy goodness topped with rich chocolate and piled with chunky candy bars on top—using the convenience of store-bought ingredients! These treats will do the trick for amped-up everyday hospitality.

6 tablespoons salted butter

1 (10-ounce) bag mini marshmallows, divided

1 teaspoon vanilla extract

6 cups Rice Krispies cereal

2 ½ cups chopped candy bars of your choice (I use Snickers or Reese's Peanut Butter Cups)

-FOR THE CHOCOLATE LAYER-

1 ½ cups milk chocolate chips

1 tablespoon solid coconut oil (do not substitute!)

Line an 8 x 8-inch or 9 x 9-inch square pan with parchment paper; set aside. In a large saucepan over medium-low heat, melt the butter. Stir in *all but 1 cup* of the mini marshmallows until melted. Remove from the heat and stir in the vanilla. Then stir in the crisped rice cereal and the remaining one cup of mini marshmallows. Stir to coat.

Pour cereal mixture into the prepared dish and use greased fingers to *gently* press into the pan. Do not mash down the layer—it will make the treats dense and not fluffy.

Working quickly, in a microwave-safe bowl, combine the milk chocolate chips and the tablespoon of coconut oil. Microwave for one minute, stir, and return to the microwave for another 20 seconds or so, stirring until melted and smooth. Repeat another 10 seconds if needed. Drizzle the chocolate evenly over the top of the marshmallow treats and use an offset spatula or utensil to carefully spread it around to create an especially sticky layer to hold the candy on. Evenly distribute the chopped candy bars over the top, gently pressing into the melted chocolate layer.

Refrigerate the pan for *no more than* 20 minutes to advance the firming up of the melted chocolate layer. Then cover airtight and store at room temperature until serving, for about 24 hours at most. Cut into 9 big squares and replace any chunky candy bar bits that may have fallen off.

CHAPTER 5

serve: the operation

*L*et's take a moment to review where we've been. We'll catch our breath, refresh our vision, and forge onward!

We each have a calling on our lives to tell our faith stories, to "shine among them" like beacons of light to the world, holding "firmly to the word of life" (Philippians 2:15–16). The way we live our lives should put God's heart on display! In Romans 12:13, Paul told us one way we should do that: *practice hospitality*. But it's in 1 Peter 4:8–11 where the apostle Peter got to the heart of things, where we see a case for hospitality: we *love* deeply, *welcome* gladly, and *serve* faithfully.

We are commanded, above all, to love deeply those who are made in God's image, to see their worth, to show compassion, to promote peace, and to acknowledge their value. John 13:35 says the way we love people is the mark of our faith as those who are in Christ Jesus.

We're created to belong to one another, to invest in relationships, and to build community with those around us. Understanding that our homes are mission fields, not museums, we initiate fellowship with others through our glad welcome, allowing our ordinary lives to showcase God's extraordinary invitation to know and be loved by Him.

Which brings us to this point—the call to serve. We're exhorted to live in a way that exemplifies Christ's love and sacrifice for His beloved humanity. Serving faithfully requires us to surrender all that we have to the purposes of the Lord God, manifesting itself in generosity and good deeds shown to all. When Christians offer their hearts, their holy welcomes, and their homes to God in order to share His heart with the world, the wonder of biblical hospitality takes place.

♥ ♥ ♥

In our headfirst dive into the hospitality commands and how-tos of 1 Peter 4:8–11, we have considered what it means to love deeply and to welcome gladly. The final hospitality command of this passage is what we'll explore in the coming pages. So gird yourself in your hardest working gear—your muck boots, your work gloves, your sweatbands and goggles—we're going in, gang. Here's the passage once more:

> Above all, love each other deeply, because love covers over a multitude of sins. Offer hospitality to one another without grumbling. Each of you should use whatever gift you have received to *serve others, as faithful stewards of God's grace* in its various forms. If anyone speaks, they should do so as one who speaks the very words of God. If anyone serves, they should do so with the strength God provides, so that in all things God may be praised

through Jesus Christ. To him be the glory and the power for ever and ever. Amen.

In regard to biblical hospitality, if *love* is the motivation and *welcome* is the invitation, then *serve* is the operation. This is where the rubber meets the road, y'all. Serving requires blood, sweat, tears, time, and talent. For greater eternal purposes, we sacrifice our lives. And if you welcome teenagers into your home, you also sacrifice your rugs, your lampshades, your sheetrock, and most of your upholstered furniture.

If you've yet to experience the serving of teenagers inside the walls of your home, let me tell you a short story.

I had just gotten two new sofas for the big family room we had built with the hopes of becoming "the house"—you know, the house where all the preteens and teens and college students want to be. I bought red couches, against my personal preference, because I expected they'd be most likely to hide stains. And not three weeks into my new couches' lives, at a gathering of teenagers, two kids collided with Styrofoam bowls of chili in their hands. Do I need to say anything further? Couches + chili + collision = sacrifice. For the record, no color or pattern on God's great planet Earth can hold its own against a chili-bowl collision.

And while I internalized my grief and grumbling as I sprayed, wiped, and did my darndest to restore those bad boys, I never once considered closing my doors or ceasing to serve. Why? Because in view of God's mercy, I offer my life, and yes, even my couches, as sacrifices for the sake of making Him known.

I did, however, consider chili in the hands of unchaperoned teenagers a no-go for the rest of my days. Amen.

♥ ♥ ♥

There is always a cost associated with serving, whether caring for babies in the nursery or going on an overseas mission trip. Whether rallying moms to provide treats for the classroom party or rallying donors to give to the building campaign. In almost all instances when we serve others, we're required to give of ourselves—our time, our plans, our money, our resources, and more.

Let's talk about our time and our plans. We sure value them, don't we? They're so important to us that we download fancy calendar apps and buy personalized paper planners with colored pens and sticky notes to color-code the fullness of our days. But when we choose to follow the Lord with a lifestyle of everyday hospitality, His plan to use us in the lives of others becomes our priority. Our plans shift from me-centered to others-centered. We can certainly mark our calendars with our favorite entertainment and pastimes— workout and coffee, hair and nails, Netflix and Hulu, tennis and Target—but we should also recognize the value of making room for others. Our availability and our willingness to serve others communicates that they matter to us and to God. Titus 3:1 tells believers "to be ready to do whatever is good." The word *ready* means to be available for any activity, action, or situation. If we want to be used by God, then we should be ready to sacrifice our plans and our time to serve others the way Christ would serve them.

Serving others not only costs us our time and plans, but it also has a financial cost. When we open our homes to people around us, it requires the sharing of our money and our resources. Hebrews 13:16 affirms this, saying, "And do not forget to do good and to share with others, for with such sacrifices God is pleased." Sharing with others is declared a sacrifice! And sacrifices come with a cost.

I don't know if you know this, but buying groceries is a sacrifice. Cereal and granola bars, sandwich bread and spreads, tenderloin and arugula, sugar, flour, milk, and eggs. Paper goods, cleaners, trash bags, and more! Plus what feels like $8 million dollars in pizza rolls and ranch dressing if you serve preteen boys. I've never had a Walmart cashier tell me that my grocery bill was on the house since I was buying it all to do good works. And the cost can certainly rack up, y'all. To say we've worn a path to our Sam's Club for big bulk buys is an understatement. But we buy the things and put in the work for this reason: How can God turn soup things into spiritual things if we aren't willing to purchase the ingredients and extend the invitation?

I told you earlier in this book that we had just moved into a new-to-us house after having sold my children's "childhood memories." When we were getting that house ready to sell after twelve years of raising our children and hosting many of their friends, we were overwhelmed by the memories of having a full house. Not only in sentimental ways but in tangible ones too! We patched the sheetrock where guys had thrown a golf ball into the wall. We repaired a toilet that had finally waved the white flag of surrender, having been destroyed by our favorite offensive lineman on the high school football team. I Magic-Erasered smudged-fingerprint grime off the cased opening between the back door and the kitchen, where years of kids had entered, jumped, and slapped when they came in. I treated the carpet in my daughter's room in front of her standing floor mirror where girls had dropped and smeared more makeup than could've possibly made it on their faces. I painted over what looked like CoverGirl TruBlend in warm beige that had been splashed, then wiped, into the sheetrock around the guest bath sink from one of the homecoming, prom, or senior picture let's-get-ready-togethers.

After the walls had been repaired, the trim had been wiped clean, and the makeup stains had been addressed, we moved out the furniture, leaving only the rug in the main gathering room where endless kids had been. It was in the basement playroom with stained concrete floors that Sam and I had built when our kids were only eight, ten, and twelve. In the coming season with teenagers, we wanted to be the house where kids hung out. We had even prayed over the foundation when it was being poured that God would make it so. And it became our greatest joy to be that house for so many years.

And that rug in the basement playroom had seen it all. Twelve years of after-parties. Twelve years of sleepovers. Twelve years of movie nights. Twelve years of drop-bys-and-stays. Twelve years of Wii, Xbox, and *Dance Dance Revolution*. Twelve years of kids sleeping on every couch, in every chair, and on every surface—including the treadmill. Twelve years of watch parties, snow days, and Friday nights. Twelve years of Grace's, Luke's, and Isaac's student ministry Bible studies that we hosted every Wednesday for what seemed like forever.

The rug was covered in stains, including orange Crush and busted pens, blood from who knows what, and, well, chili. I knew it had given all it had for the cause, so I got on my knees to roll it up and haul it off.

As I began to roll the rug, it disintegrated before my eyes. It actually became like dust! It cracked instead of rolled. It unraveled and tore in my hands. At first I shrieked in disbelief. I sent a video to my kids of what had become of the rug, and we all got a big laugh. But as I sat on my knees with that threadbare, deteriorated rug in my hands, I cried my face off. All the years, the lives, the hearts, the ministry. All the nights of hot dogs, board games, and circle-up-and-prays. That rug was a mark of valor, a battleground scar.

That rug was holy ground.

Serving requires sacrifice. It costs us plenty. But do you know what? We consider it absolutely worth it. Because for us, there's no investment too high that would keep us from enabling an encounter between God and His people.

I'm not saying that Sam and I are holier than you or that we have it all together. And we certainly don't have a massive bankroll we can just spend without a care in the world. The reason we place such value on serving others through acts of welcome and time around our table is because we love God, we want people to know that love, and we've experienced firsthand the sweet ministry that happens when we use our home to share His heart with others. It's really that simple.

Follow me here. When we surrender our lives to Christ through faith, the things we once believed were ours, we now consider His. It's no longer *my* time, *my* calendar, or *my* bank account; instead, they belong to Him. Then God takes those sacrifices and uses them for eternal purposes in the lives of those around us, and they feel less like sacrifices and more like offerings of worship. They no longer feel like something we *have* to give up. The Lord turns our reluctance into readiness and our wavering into willingness! Then our willingness increases our welcome. He changes our perspective, turning our clinched and greedy hands into generous ones that hold loosely to our time, resources, and lives.

I just love that word *generous*! What does it mean to be generous? The *Oxford Dictionary* defines *generous* as "showing a readiness to give more of something, as money or time, than is strictly necessary or expected."[1] Do you see the concept of readiness again here? Titus 3:1, Hebrews 10:24–25, and even the *Oxford Dictionary* all affirm the idea of being ready—ready to do good works, prepared to share and serve, and ready to give away more than is expected!

Having a spirit of generosity empowers us to serve. Often we use *generosity* and *kindness* interchangeably; however, they are different in a very specific way. The main difference between kindness and generosity is that kindness refers to being friendly and thinking about other people's feelings, while generosity is associated with a person's willingness to give something to another—sharing liberally what they have. Don't we desire to be generous people—generous with our time and talent, our hearts and homes, our Friday nights and our faith stories—sharing graciously all that we have in order for people to know the love of the Lord? That, my dear ones, is the soul of biblical hospitality.

♥ ♥ ♥

When Sam and I were in our midtwenties, we were on the receiving end of this kind of service and generous hospitality. We had been married about three years, and I was pregnant with our second baby. Our *second* baby, gang. Our first baby came only seventeen months after our wedding day. So, if I'm doing the math for you, I was twenty-five, six months pregnant, and I had an eighteen-month-old at home. I think they call that "babies having babies." Sam was the new youth pastor at Fellowship Bible Church of Northwest Arkansas, helping rebuild a student ministry. We were in full swing, investing in the lives of other peoples' babies while we made and raised our own.

One afternoon when Sam was playing basketball with some students, he suffered a major knee injury. So major that when he was driven home by friends and carried inside, his complexion was pea-soup green. We learned via MRI that he had fundamentally destroyed all cartilage and ligaments and everything in between, which would require nuts and bolts and screws across two surgeries over twelve weeks. He was immobile, flat on his back, only crutched upright for the most urgent things.

A few weeks into Sam's surgeries and recovery process, I was put on bed rest. *Bed rest.* This meant both parents were on our backs, in the bed, unable to cook or clean or care for our toddler. We learned very quickly that an eighteen-month-old on the loose was like a little baby ninja. She amazed us with her ability to scale walls, hot-wire cars, and open canned goods. My parents were kind enough to take our ninja baby for a week until things settled, but we were both still entirely horizontal. We were young, scared, and wondered at times if God had forgotten about us.

But the body of Christ served us in the most generous way! Women in the church showed up night after night to bring us food, to care for us, and to feed us body and soul. The wife of one of our pastors, affectionately known by all as Sweet Anne, brought us creamy chicken enchiladas and spinach salad with strawberries, red onions, and pecans. Our friend Barbi brought us fried chicken tenders and sweet potato fries in a Styrofoam clamshell from the restaurant she and her husband had just opened. And knowing that I loved their homemade blueberry poppy seed dressing, she came with a *vat* of it in hand as well! Our pediatrician's wife and dear friend, Julia, came to our door with a piping hot chicken pot pie, the aroma of which will surely welcome us at the gates of heaven. And my friend and mentor Sue (aka "wife of sock-feet Tom") brought us a comforting casserole—*and she took our laundry*, washing, folding, and returning it to us a day later. I'm here to tell you that nothing says "desperate" like letting someone else wash your panties!

These women of faith offered up their gifts, time, and resources to love us well. Sure, they had housefuls of kids at the prime of activity. They had responsibilities, jobs, parents to care for, Bible studies to prepare, toilets to clean, and their own families to feed. But they sacrificed—they *offered*—all that they had to become Jesus to us. At a time when we were afraid and felt forgotten, their hospitality allowed us to feel God's touch in our lives. He became tangible. He became palpable. He became real.

Why did they serve us that way? Why should *we* serve others in the same way? Because we're called to love deeply, welcome gladly, and serve faithfully, demonstrating God's heart to the world.

And let me make an important observation: when these women served us, they not only impacted our lives for the long haul, but they impacted their children's lives as well. All four households modeled for their children what everyday hospitality looks like. We were only one family who was on the receiving end of their faithfulness and generosity. But Anne, Barbi, Julia, and Sue have opened their doors and lives, met needs, and shared the love of God with countless others over all the years. And do you know what? Now their adult children and grandchildren do the same. They say more is caught than is taught, and biblical hospitality is no different. Whether greedy or giving hands, stingy or shared lives, we can influence the ones who follow behind us and the ones after them. May all who come behind us find us faithful, and may we be people who cultivate generations of generosity.

♥ ♥ ♥

Servanthood is at the heart of the Christian faith. How do we know? Because the one we follow, Jesus Christ, not only taught about servant-hood but He also modeled it in life and, ultimately, death. Jesus said this about servanthood in Mark 10:43–45:

> Whoever wants to become great among you must be your servant, and whoever wants to be first must be slave of all. For even the Son of Man did not come to be served, but to serve, and to give his life as a ransom for many.

Though He was the King of glory, who deserved ovation and laud, pomp and circumstance, honor and praise, instead He became the ultimate servant and gave His life away. Christ came to serve, and we should live in the same way. Jesus taught that true greatness is found in giving of oneself for the sake of others.

In Philippians 2:3–8, Paul affirmed these notions in a decidedly compelling passage regarding Christ's incredible example of sacrifice and our call to imitate Him in our lives.

> Do nothing out of selfish ambition or vain conceit. Rather, in humility value others above yourselves, not looking to your own interests but each of you to the interests of the others. In your relationships with one another, have the same mindset as Christ Jesus:
>
> > Who, being in very nature God,
> > did not consider equality with God something to be
> > used to his own advantage;
> > rather, he made himself nothing
> > by taking the very nature of a servant,
> > being made in human likeness.
> > And being found in appearance as a man,
> > he humbled himself
> > by becoming obedient to death—
> > even death on a cross!

We marvel at our Lord's humility, His lowliness. The King became a servant. Our everything became nothing. He gave all that He had as the ultimate sacrifice to satisfy the internal nothingness and eternal need of humanity.

In Philippians and throughout Scripture, we are called to be imitators of Christ; we're encouraged to consider others better than ourselves—better than our plans, better than our money, better than our opinions, and better than our time. Serving requires us to lay down our lives for others the way Christ laid down His life for us.

In Jerusalem, only hours before His crucifixion, Christ gathered His disciples for a final meal together in the upper room. Sharing bread and wine at the Last Supper, Jesus explained that the elements were symbols of His body and blood that would be given as ransom for their lives, the forgiveness of their sins. In John 13, we see that Jesus got up during the meal, took the role of a servant, filled a basin with water, and washed the disciples' feet, using His own towel to dry them. It's important to understand that the act of foot washing was usually carried out by slaves, and those who received the foot washing were considered superior to those who were offering the service. So on the very rare occasion that the host extended the service, it indicated deep love and devotion.

With all the social implications of this act of service, the disciples were caught off guard and uncomfortable when Jesus washed their feet. Simon Peter even objected, telling the Lord that He should never be the one to wash his feet. Can you blame Simon Peter? I mean, can you imagine this monumental reversal of roles? The King of kings taking the lowliest place? The Lord of lords kneeling before *you*, washing *your* feet, serving *you*?

Not only did Jesus perform this loving and lowly act for His disciples but He also followed with a command for how they should likewise live their lives. John 13:14–15 says, "Now that I, your Lord and Teacher, have washed your feet, you also should wash one another's feet. I have set you an example that you should do as I have done for you." Jesus told them that what He did for them, they should likewise do for others.

Last night. Last words. Lasting image. Wash one another's feet.

♥ ♥ ♥

Serving others the way Christ called us to serve is counterintuitive. We aren't born wishing to put others before ourselves. Just think about the behavior of children! They want what they want, when they want it, and how they want it. And if they don't get it, then there's thrashing and carrying on, pouting, biting, and hitting someone with whatever's in hand at the time.

Although our outward behavior may change as we grow up, our inner desire to please "self" doesn't. We may no longer hit people on top of the head with a board book, but our selfish desires still blur our vision, steer our ships, and rule our lives. Without Christ in our lives, without giving Him a rightful place as Lord, we still look out for number one. Why wouldn't we? However, when we surrender our lives in faith to the lordship of Christ, the Spirit of God comes to dwell in us. We're given a new heart. Our minds are renewed and transformed. And Christ's intuition to serve others becomes ours.

Not only is God-inspired service counterintuitive, but it's countercultural. We live in a "me first" world. Y'all, the culture we live in grieves me so. Without considering you one bit, people will climb over, slander, and mash you to a pulp in order to get what they want or to be on top. We see needs but look away. The hurts and heartbreak of those around us fall on deaf ears. Others' calamities cramp our style. Their distress dampens our days. Their relational needs really ask too much of our time. Most people serve themselves first, others if it's convenient, and God maybe.

But Christianity reverses the order of value! Followers of Jesus turn this ideology upside down when we put God first, others second, and ourselves last. Then when people of faith who are marked by the love of Christ serve others, it causes those whose eyes are on self to look at us and see Jesus. Our lives look so utterly different from what they're accustomed to seeing that they can't help but curiously take note. Matthew 5:16 declares, "Let your light shine before others, that they may see your good deeds and glorify your Father in heaven." We showcase the heart of God to a watching world when we give of ourselves for the sake of others.

♥ ♥ ♥

Jennifer and her husband are walking through a disappointing season of infertility. If you've found yourself on the same journey, then you know there are daily occurrences that remind you that you're not yet a parent. Jennifer confessed it's a struggle being both sad and mad that she's not a mama while still being genuinely excited for people who are celebrating their new lives with little ones. Through the frustration of this time, Jennifer has felt God teaching her to serve *anyway*. Through her heartbreak and tears, the Lord has been nudging her to love and serve the expectant mamas in her life.

Recently, one of her dearest friends, who was thirty-nine weeks pregnant and exhausted, mentioned that she needed to get groceries for some slow cooker meals that week. Prompted by the Holy Spirit (the one who replaces your intuition with God's intuition), Jennifer asked her friend if she had freezer space, sensing in that moment the call to love and serve her friend. So Jennifer planned to make three meals for them in order for this new little family to be fed when they got home from the hospital: Italian chicken sliders, white chicken lasagna, and southwestern taco bake.

The following night, Jennifer spent a couple of hours in the kitchen prepping, chopping, stirring, assembling, and wrapping meals. And while she worked, she prayed. She prayed for God to bless her friend's growing family, for happiness and health, grace and favor. Jennifer would tell you that those prayers were as much for her as they were for her friends. In those moments, she realized she could desperately desire something that someone else was being blessed with, while loving and serving that person with a glad heart anyway. Jennifer loved others deeply, humbly served her friend's family, and gladly laid down her life, showing them God's heart through her hospitality.

First John 3:16–18 tells us,

This is how we know what love is: Jesus Christ laid down his life for us. And we ought to lay down our lives for our brothers and sisters. If anyone has material possessions and sees a brother or sister in need but has no pity on them, how can the love of God be in that person? Dear children, let us not love with words or speech but with actions and in truth.

"Let us not love with words or speech but with actions and in truth." Simply stated: loving and serving go hand in hand. If God's people love people, then God's people serve people. You see, love is more than a feeling, more than an idea, more than intention. Love is more than well-wishing or expressing concern. It moves. It gestures. It acts. Bob Goff explained in his book *Love Does*, "Love is never stationary. In the end, love doesn't just keep thinking about it or keep planning for it. Simply put: love does."[2] The depth of love we're encouraged to show throughout Scripture moves beyond, "I'm so glad you're in our neighborhood" and, "I'm so sorry to hear that!" Love moves to action.

Love goes to the grocery store. Love takes out the trash. It drives a meal across town. Love vacuums and dusts. Love sweeps the porch. It runs errands on behalf of others. Love pours coffee and steeps tea. Love hosts an elderly neighbor or a gaggle of giggling girls. Love loads the dishwasher. It sets a table or counts paper plates. Love picks up a pizza. Love sears meat and roasts carrots. Love folds towels and washes sheets. Love leans in, speaks with grace, and prays. Love opens the door. Love welcomes. And love serves.

In 1 John 3:17, quoted on the previous page, we saw these words: "If anyone has material possessions and sees a brother or sister in need but has no pity on them, how can the love of God be in that person?" How can people who say they love God see emotional and physical needs of those around them and not be moved to action? John said they can't, or the love of God isn't truly in them. With respect to biblical hospitality, we can translate 1 John 3:17 this way: "What good does it do to have the means and the time to make a few freezer meals if you don't prepare them for a pregnant friend?" "What good does it do to have the ingredients for soup in your pantry if you don't make it and share it with your grieving neighbor?" "What good does it do to have a guest room if you don't turn down the sheets and invite someone to stay?"

Here's the bottom line, friends. If we say we love God and we claim that His love is in us, then we serve others. God's people love people. And God's people *serve*.

♥ ♥ ♥

Food for Thought

- ♥ If serving equals sacrifice, then what does serving others through acts of hospitality cost us? What is the most difficult sacrifice for you? Time? Money and resources? What else?
- ♥ How is serving others counterintuitive? How is serving others countercultural? How can our counterintuitive and counter-cultural service display Christ to the world?

♥ How was Christ's washing His disciples' feet an example for us to follow? What does it require of our hearts to be able to serve in such a way?

♥ What is your favorite way to serve others through hospitality? When have you laid down your life for the sake of others and the Lord blessed you in return?

♥ ♥ ♥

chicken pot pie in a pinch

SERVES 6

In my cookbook Love Welcome Serve: Recipes that Gather and Give, *there's a lengthy-but-worth-it recipe for Comfort Chicken Pot Pie that is rich and filling and oh-so-good. You can certainly make the lengthy version in my cookbook; however, this recipe is the one my friend Julia brought to Sam and me during our shared season of bed rest and despair. It uses store-bought shortcuts, it requires no laborious chopping or sautéing, and it tastes like the love of Jesus just the same!*

1 box (2-count) premade refrigerated pie crusts

2 ½ cups shredded cooked chicken

1 (29-ounce) can Veg-All homestyle large cut vegetables, drained

1 (14.5-ounce) can cream of chicken soup

3–4 teaspoons Cavender's All Purpose Greek Seasoning to taste

Salt and pepper to taste

1 egg white + 1 teaspoon of water for brushing crust, optional

Preheat the oven to 375°F. Remove the box of pie crusts from the refrigerator and let them sit on the counter in their plastic sleeves while you prep the rest. About 10 minutes on the counter will allow the crusts to unroll easier.

In a big bowl, combine the shredded chicken, drained vegetables, and canned soup. Season with Cavender's, stirring to combine. Taste and adjust, adding salt and pepper if needed. Place a bottom crust in a standard 9-inch pie plate, pour in the filling, and top with the second crust; crimp together to seal.

In a small bowl, splash the egg white with water, stir together, and brush the top of the crust with the egg wash. Poke holes in the top with a fork or cut decorative slits to allow pie to vent steam. Sprinkle the top crust with a little salt and pepper. Bake for 35 to 45 minutes or until golden and bubbly. Cover the top loosely with foil if it starts looking a little too brown. Allow to cool about 10 minutes before cutting and serving.

notes

- ♥ You can certainly use pulled meat from a rotisserie chicken, but it may add a smokier and saltier taste. Be sure to adjust salt and seasonings accordingly.
- ♥ I added the option of brushing the top crust with egg wash, but it's not necessary! An egg wash just makes the crust especially golden and pretty.
- ♥ Use a standard pie dish, not a deep dish, or your pot pie will not fill the dish. Also remember to keep foil pie pans in stock so you can easily make and give them away!
- ♥ You can give this pot pie assembled with instructions for baking. You can give this pot pie fully baked for easy reheating. Or you can give a pot pie frozen with instructions to bake from the freezer. (In a 375°F oven, bake for 30 minutes covered with foil; remove foil and bake another 25 to 30 minutes or until golden, bubbly, and piping hot in the center.)
- ♥ Julia sends this pot pie with a big jar of chunky applesauce or store-bought cinnamon apples. I do the same!

christ-centered hospitality

CHAPTER 6

jesus: the model

*I*f we are called to practice hospitality and to model the life of Christ, then it would be fitting to examine how Jesus used the ministry of hospitality in His own life, right? Consider how many times the Bible tells the story of people encountering Christ at the table, in their homes, or over a shared meal.

In his book *A Meal with Jesus,* Tim Chester lists multiple accounts in the gospel of Luke alone in which Jesus ate with people:

Luke 5: Jesus ate with tax collectors and sinners at Levi's house.

Luke 7: Jesus accepted an invitation to eat in the home of Simon the Pharisee.

Luke 9: Jesus fed a crowd of five thousand-plus.

Luke 10: Jesus was welcomed in the home of Mary and Martha for a meal and a stay.

Luke 11: Jesus was reclined at the Pharisee's table when He
warned the teachers of the law.

Luke 14: Jesus was at a meal when He said that welcoming the
broken results in blessing.

Luke 19: Jesus initiated hospitality by coming to Zaccheaus's
house.

Luke 22: Jesus gathered His nearest and dearest around a table
for the Last Supper.[1]

And that's not all! The woman at the well, the wedding at Cana,
plus countless parables, narratives, comparisons, and more are food-
focused in the Scriptures. Feasts, the Bread of Life, living water, and
I could go on and on!

The array of people Christ engaged in hospitality is broad. What
a mixed bag! Becoming the talk of the town, He broke bread with
tax collectors and sinners. He hung out with people who were distant from God. He shared meals with people whose bad reputations
had spread far and wide. These meals drew the controversial opinions and judgment of some. "How can He dine with people like
that?" they would say. "Doesn't He know what kind of woman she
is?" they would scoff.

On the other end of the spiritual spectrum, Jesus also gathered
around a table with distinguished religious leaders and Pharisees, who
were the legal experts of the day. These dinners usually included some
heated conversation about the truths of the kingdom of God and the
condition of their hearts. Jesus not only engaged heaven's outsiders
and holy rollers, but He also dined with His disciples and supporters,
His nearest and dearest, His friends and companions. He attended
weddings, funerals, and banquets. On most occasions, Jesus was on
the receiving end of a hospitality invitation, but there are accounts
where Christ did, in fact, play the role of dinner host and even chef!

The Bible tells us in Matthew 11:19, "The Son of Man came eating and drinking." Why is that? Because Jesus knew there was something significant about what happens around the table. He knew that a simple act of hospitality created the perfect platform for emotional, relational, and spiritual transactions to take place. For Jesus, the table was a primary platform for ministry, not because He was a foodie but because He was a people person. And He knew what my grandmother Euna Mae knew—that food was a means to an end, and the end was demonstrating the goodness of God in the lives of others. Breaking bread and sharing the cup allowed Jesus to find common ground with people from all walks of life, from all socioeconomic levels, and from all spiritual conditions. Jesus used the intimacy of a shared meal to express truth and grace. He used the ordinary of the table to impart His extraordinary love and care.

It was in this way that Rosaria Butterfield's life was completely changed. Through the faithful, generous hospitality extended to her by neighbors who knew Christ, she came to understand God's great plan for her life. She went on to pen *The Gospel Comes with a House Key* about the Lord's capturing her heart over years of hospitality shown by her believing friends. She considers that hospitality is ground zero for the Christian faith, saying, "Hospitality, biblically speaking, takes strangers and makes them neighbors, and takes neighbors and makes them family of God."[2] Jesus knew this. He modeled this!

Christ used the most basic, ordinary, daily activity of eating a meal as a primary tool for meeting emotional and spiritual needs. He invited people to gather, feeding and nourishing them. He loved, welcomed, and served. Christ strategically used the ministry of hospitality in all kinds of ways with all kinds of folks to bring about restoration and inspiration. Over the setting of a meal, He evangelized and discipled, confronted and corrected both the lost and the found. People were not only filled but they were also satisfied. And their lives were never the same. In this chapter, we will look at a few engagements with Jesus at the table.

♥ ♥ ♥

In Luke 5:27–32, we see Jesus at the table with sinners.

> After this, Jesus went out and saw a tax collector by the name of Levi sitting at his tax booth. "Follow me," Jesus said to him, and Levi got up, left everything and followed him. Then Levi held a great banquet for Jesus at his house, and a large crowd of tax collectors and others were eating with them. But the Pharisees and the teachers of the law who belonged to their sect complained to his disciples, "Why do you eat and drink with tax collectors and sinners?" Jesus answered them, "It is not the healthy who need a doctor, but the sick. I have not come to call the righteous, but sinners to repentance."

Levi was a tax collector turned Christ follower. In recent days, Levi had experienced a radical conversion, responding to the call of Christ in his life. So he left everything behind to follow the great Teacher who had changed everything for him. Levi left behind his position, his title, and his old ways. With a new leader, new values, and a new purpose, Levi had become a new man!

For your understanding and for all the accountants reading this, let me explain why Levi's having been a tax collector equated him with being a sinner. In biblical times, tax collectors weren't considered honest folk. They were greedy, dishonest, and often took entirely more than they should. They took advantage of their position by taking advantage of the people around them. And because tax collectors in Israel were most often Jews who worked for the Romans, they were considered traitors.

As a sinner on the other side of repentance, Levi wanted to express his newfound love for the Lord Jesus, so he held a banquet to celebrate his new Teacher and the new life he had found in Him! It wasn't just a casual get-together; no, the Bible describes it as a *great* banquet! Having a career as a tax collector would mean that Levi was a man of reasonable fortune, so this gathering would've been a night to remember. It also would imply that not only his new friends in the faith would be attending but also his cronies from his tax-collecting days. You've likely found yourself at a gathering with similarly polar-opposite people. Can you imagine what this event was like? What did they talk about? Did the guests curb their conversation out of respect for the holy man in their midst? Or did they let loose with topics and tenor that were true to form? Was Levi embarrassed by his old friends in front of his new King? How did Jesus interact with Levi's friends? Did the guest of honor leave early or linger into the night?

We don't know exactly how that evening went down or what took place at Levi's house. Scripture doesn't say. But we do know that Jesus was in the business of using the table as a bridge to build relationships in order to reach the lost. He was known for creating common ground to lead to higher ground. After all, both sinners and rabbis alike have to eat, right?

Although the goings-on at the banquet are not revealed, the purpose of Christ's accepting the invitation to dine with sinners is revealed. In Luke 5:30, the religious elite known as the Pharisees questioned Jesus' followers. In my best southern mother translation: "For cryin' out loud! Why on earth is He hangin' out with all those heathens? Didn't His Daddy teach Him any better?" *clutches pearls*

Without missing a beat, Jesus declared that He came to call sinners to repentance. To heal them of their sickness—that is, their sin. To offer them the life-changing, course-altering hope that Levi found. To save their souls.

The Pharisees couldn't fathom why Jesus would gather or break bread with people who lived so utterly opposite of what He believed and taught. They assumed that sharing a meal with them was equivalent with accepting and approving of the lifestyles that filled the room. But dear ones, Jesus wasn't approving sin or promoting sin. His proximity came with a purpose. His meals were missional. Christ said He came to seek and save that which was lost. And one of the ways He did that was to break bread, drawing near to those far from God.

♥ ♥ ♥

Not only did Jesus engage in hospitality with sinful people who knew they were far from God, but He also dined with religious people who were equally distant from God—they just didn't realize it. Jesus used hospitality moments to spend intentional time with both the righteous and unrighteous, the holy rollers and the sinners.

In Luke 7, 11, and 14, we see Jesus accepted invitations to dine with Pharisees and experts of the law. These invitations were extended by religious leaders who were considered polarizing figures in the community. You see, Pharisees were known for their self-righteous demeanors, expressed in their extreme rules for pious living. They drew hard lines in the sand with their stands for right and wrong. And in their eyes, mostly everyone was on the wrong side of that line—except for themselves, of course. Of all the kinds of people with whom Jesus interacted, He was likely the hardest on the Pharisees. Their judgmental extremism and legalistic interpretations of God's law were out of bounds in the eyes of the Lord.

So what did Christ do about them? How did He respond to these holy rollers? He joined them on common ground. He accepted their invitations to break bread, to share a meal with them. Jesus engaged them in acts of hospitality time and time again. He dined with the opposition. He ate with people who hoped for Him to fail.

Naturally, Jesus' dinners with the Pharisees were not without controversy or tension. In each instance, pleasantries would move to confrontational instruction. Jesus would shift from common ground to battleground, revealing realities about the kingdom of God. But in order to crack their sanctimonious shells, He broke bread with them first.

In Luke 7, Jesus dined at the home of Simon the Pharisee. And during the dinner, an uninvited and certainly unexpected guest showed up. A woman with a scandalous reputation crashed the party. Was she a prostitute? A mistress? A woman who moved from bed to bed? Imagine the scene—the significant lifestyle extremes in the same room at the same time. A Pharisee and a prostitute. A man known for his piety and a woman notorious for her promiscuity were at the same dinner party with Jesus. While Simon the Pharisee watched in judgment what was happening before him, the woman knelt and wept tears on Christ's feet, using her hair to wipe His feet as she anointed them with oil.

What happened next was a lesson on forgiveness and the value of our heart-position before God, as Jesus addressed the two postures in the room. Christ took the opportunity to teach a houseful of observers what it looks like to be right before the Lord: humble, seeking, empty, broken, surrendered. The context of hospitality enabled the encounter. Bites of food led to bits of truth.

Likewise, in Luke 11 and 14, we see Jesus dined with Pharisees as their invited guest, using the table as His pulpit to teach the words of life. Over and over, Jesus demonstrated that these shared occasions in homes or at tables gained Him an audience with those who would not normally seek to sit under His teaching, even though they were the very ones who needed to hear it! The commonality of food and hunger, plus the simple pleasure of gathering, was used for kingdom purposes.

From where He was seated, Jesus brought truth through His presence and His words. His conversation moved beyond the weather and the wall color to some pretty important discussion of doctrine and godly living. With the religious leaders, Jesus addressed hypocrisy, pride, and ignoring the needs of the poor. Heavy stuff, y'all! But with grace, Jesus revealed the will of the Father to His most holy hosts as well as the others in the room.

♥ ♥ ♥

In Luke 19:1–10, we see Jesus at the table with Zacchaeus, a spiritual seeker.

> Jesus entered Jericho and was passing through. A man was there by the name of Zacchaeus; he was a chief tax collector and was wealthy. He wanted to see who Jesus was, but because he was short he could not see over the crowd. So he ran ahead and climbed a sycamore-fig tree to see him, since Jesus was coming that way.
>
> When Jesus reached the spot, he looked up and said to him, "Zacchaeus, come down immediately. I must stay at your house today." So he came down at once and welcomed him gladly.
>
> All the people saw this and began to mutter, "He has gone to be the guest of a sinner."

But Zacchaeus stood up and said to the Lord, "Look, Lord! Here and now I give half of my possessions to the poor, and if I have cheated anybody out of anything, I will pay back four times the amount."

Jesus said to him, "Today salvation has come to this house, because this man, too, is a son of Abraham. For the Son of Man came to seek and to save the lost."

Jesus most often played the role of invited guest when we see Him in various hospitality situations in Scripture, but in Luke 19, Jesus initiated hospitality by inviting Himself over to do an in-home visit of sorts with a man who was seeking God. You see, Jesus lived much of His ministry on the road, city to city, shore to shore. He didn't officially have a place to call home. He even claimed about Himself in Matthew 8:20 that "the Son of Man has no place to lay his head." So when presented with an opportunity to create common ground, to build a relationship, to invest in a life, He suggested they go to Zacchaeus's home instead!

Oh, the encouragement we see here to seize hospitality opportunities whenever and however we can! Sure, Jesus could've shared truth right there on the spot or in a dozen other places, but He knew there was something sacred and set apart about crossing the threshold of someone's home. It's intimate, vulnerable, and real. It's inviting and familiar. And in this case, it was the ideal setting for Christ to have a heart-to-heart conversation with a man who was curious about God.

You see, Zacchaeus was a short man with a tall reputation. He was influential and affluent, but his wealth came to him by dishonest means. Like Levi, he was a tax collector—and not just any tax collector, he was chief among them. Filling his bank account by cheating those around him had robbed Zacchaeus of any meaningful relationships. He was rich but not generous. He was a greedy, sinful man, and everyone knew it, including Jesus.

So in Luke 19, when Zacchaeus displayed spiritual interest by climbing a tree to get a good look at Jesus over the crowd, Christ seized the opportunity. He recognized this tax collector's need as well as the spiritual interest that God was stirring inside him, so He invited Himself over! Think about what it means that Zacchaeus gladly accepted. He opened his door to Jesus and hosted Him. Imagine how lonely he likely had been, how long it may have been since anyone had wanted to come over. He was surely in need of relationships—this one in particular.

Now the Bible doesn't tell us exactly what happened, whether they shared a meal or just had tea, but we know that after Zacchaeus encountered Christ in his own home, his life was changed. He announced his repentance, and Jesus announced that salvation had come to his house. Zacchaeus was no longer a seeker; he was saved.

♥ ♥ ♥

In Luke 22:8–20, we see Jesus at the table with His disciples.

Jesus sent Peter and John, saying, "Go and make preparations for us to eat the Passover."

"Where do you want us to prepare for it?" they asked.

He replied, "As you enter the city, a man carrying a jar of water will meet you. Follow him to the house that he enters, and say to the owner of the house, 'The Teacher asks: Where is the guest room, where I may eat the Passover with my disciples?' He will show you a large room upstairs, all furnished. Make preparations there."

They left and found things just as Jesus had told them. So they prepared the Passover.

When the hour came, Jesus and his apostles reclined at the table. And he said to them, "I have eagerly desired to eat this Passover with you before I suffer. For I tell you, I will not eat it again until it finds fulfillment in the kingdom of God."

After taking the cup, he gave thanks and said, "Take this and divide it among you. For I tell you I will not drink again from the fruit of the vine until the kingdom of God comes."

And he took bread, gave thanks and broke it, and gave it to them, saying, "This is my body given for you; do this in remembrance of me."

In the same way, after the supper he took the cup, saying, "This cup is the new covenant in my blood, which is poured out for you."

We've seen Jesus receiving table invitations, as well as initiating a hospitality moment with a spiritual seeker, but in Luke 22, we see Jesus becoming the host. Only hours before He would be betrayed, arrested, and crucified—knowing this was His last gathering with His favored friends and most faithful followers—Jesus hosted a dinner.

We've seen that Christ used acts of hospitality as a platform for important spiritual transactions to take place. We saw it in the lives of sinners, holy rollers, and spiritual seekers. And this evening was no different! Jesus gathered His friends around a table to partake in the Seder meal in celebration of the Passover. The Passover Feast had been celebrated for hundreds of years throughout generations in remembrance of God's faithfulness to deliver Israel out of Egypt. But the Passover meal on this very night was the most significant of all time!

Known to us as the Last Supper, this was Christ's final night before His arrest and crucifixion, when He shared His last words with His disciples. You are likely familiar with this image because various representations of it are everywhere. I even have a local artist's breathtaking rendition of the Last Supper hanging in my foyer! I mean, have you ever thrown a dinner party that was given a title almost everyone on the planet recognizes, or became so legendary that it was painted by one of the world's most famous artists? Have you ever hosted a bridal luncheon that was written about by hundreds of poets throughout history? Yeah, me neither. This formal meal didn't become world-renowned because of what was *on* the table but for what happened *at* the table.

In the story, Jesus assumed the role of host. He reserved the room, pulled together a committee to help with preparations, and invited His friends. He set the menu, considering the flow of the evening as well as the content of the night. He was director of the meal and the conversation. He blessed and served the food and drink, revealing that both represented the salvation sacrifice He would soon make on behalf of their collective souls. In a wonderful preview of the gospel message, Jesus loved them, He welcomed them, and He served them. Only hours later would the symbolism of Christ's hospitality handiwork that night be manifested in the most substantive way on the cross, where Jesus loved the world sacrificially, He welcomed all who would come to Him, and He served by giving His life as a ransom for many (Mark 10:45).

Oh, the imagery of the evening! What hospitality Christ showed! An intimate invitation extended. The humblest acts shown. Powerful principles shared. Significant symbolism revealed. Jesus Christ, the Lamb of God who would take away the sin of the world, changed lives at this most famous dinner party in the history of humankind. Yours and mine included.

♥ ♥ ♥

In John 21:4–12, we see the resurrected Jesus on the shore with His broken spiritual brother, Peter:

> Early in the morning, Jesus stood on the shore, but the disciples did not realize that it was Jesus.
>
> He called out to them, "Friends, haven't you any fish?"
>
> "No," they answered.
>
> He said, "Throw your net on the right side of the boat and you will find some." When they did, they were unable to haul the net in because of the large number of fish.
>
> Then the disciple whom Jesus loved said to Peter, "It is the Lord!" As soon as Simon Peter heard him say, "It is the Lord," he wrapped his outer garment around him (for he had taken it off) and jumped into the water. The other disciples followed in the boat, towing the net full of fish, for they were not far from shore, about a hundred yards. When they landed, they saw a fire of burning coals there with fish on it, and some bread.
>
> Jesus said to them, "Bring some of the fish you have just caught." So Simon Peter climbed back into the boat and dragged the net ashore. It was full of large fish, 153, but even with so many the net was not torn. Jesus said to them, "Come and have breakfast." None of the disciples dared ask him, "Who are you?" They knew it was the Lord.

One of my favorite meals in all Scripture is found in this passage. The resurrected Christ cooked fish on the shoreline for His friends! It was a cookout, a fireside chat, or a resurrection tailgate, you might say.

After the resurrection, Jesus showed up early in the morning where His beloved Peter and several others were fishing. Jesus set up shop, took on the role as host and cook, built a fire, and grilled fish and bread on the shoreline. Envision Jesus Christ—Savior of the world, who had just conquered death—collecting sticks, stacking rocks, tending to a fire, grilling fish, and serving bread. Did He stop at a sidewalk cart in the city for groceries? Was the food provided to Him by a friend? Did He reach into a basket and supernaturally take hold of fish and loaves as He was known to do?

Upon setting the scene, Jesus called out to the disciples across the sea, beckoning them to join Him for breakfast: "Friends, come and eat!" Remember, only days earlier, Peter had denied knowing Jesus when his neck was on the line. Ponder how Peter must've felt when he realized that his Messiah, whom he had denied over and over, was inviting him to eat and calling him *friend*! I mean, in Peter's mind, he and Jesus were on the outs. Peter had likely spent the last few days beating himself up over his unwillingness to be known as Christ's friend and follower, replaying those scenes over and over with regret. How could he do such a thing to the one he had left everything to follow?

However, through Jesus' invitation to share a meal with Him, Peter's relationship with Christ was restored. Peter's shame was replaced with grace over a meal on the shore. People who are cooked for feel cared for, remember?

♥ ♥ ♥

In all these hospitality occurrences, we observe that Christ used the table as a pulpit. We see repeatedly that an invitation to share a meal or gather in the comfort of a home laid the relational groundwork for Christ to turn soup things into spiritual things. And His breakfast on the shore with Peter was no different. It was a meal that had far greater purpose than showcasing the Lord's culinary skills or showing off a net filled with wonder.

To the man who cast nets for all of his days, Jesus cast vision for the rest of Peter's life:

> When they had finished eating, Jesus said to Simon Peter, "Simon son of John, do you love me more than these?"
>
> "Yes, Lord," he said, "you know that I love you."
>
> Jesus said, "Feed my lambs."
>
> Again Jesus said, "Simon son of John, do you love me?"
>
> He answered, "Yes, Lord, you know that I love you."
>
> Jesus said, "Take care of my sheep."
>
> The third time he said to him, "Simon son of John, do you love me?"
>
> Peter was hurt because Jesus asked him the third time, "Do you love me?" He said, "Lord, you know all things; you know that I love you."
>
> Jesus said, "Feed my sheep." (John 21:15–17)

Jesus said to Peter, "Feed my sheep." In other words, "Peter, if you love Me, then you'll care well for people who are made in My image and nourish them with spiritual food. If you love Me, then you'll make known that I am the one who satisfies the thirsty and fills the hungry with good things. If you love Me, then you'll lead the ones who know Me and guide the ones who don't into the eternal fold."

In one final revealed expression of hospitality, Jesus served this missional meal. He shared food for His followers' bellies and food for their souls. He set the scene, initiated the exchange, and served a meal, turning soup things into spiritual things, casting vision for Peter and for us as well: *feed My sheep.*

Whether we are the guest, host, or cook, our shared meals can become spiritual food when we model hospitality after the One who satisfies our souls.

♥ ♥ ♥

Food for Thought

♥ Christ believed in the power of a shared meal and used the atmosphere of hospitality to turn soup things into spiritual things. What roles do we see Jesus play in these hospitality settings? With what kinds of people did Christ share a hospitality encounter?

♥ How did Jesus use the table to turn soup things into spiritual things in each of the narratives in this chapter? Have you ever experienced a dinner that ministered to your soul, where your faith was fortified, where your fellowship with others impassioned you, taught you, comforted you, or filled you with joy?

♥ What do you think Christ meant when He told Peter and the disciples to "feed my sheep" (John 21:17)? What does that look like in your life? How do you feel about using hospitality to deliver spiritual nourishment to others?

♥ ♥ ♥

pasta salad supreme

SERVES 6 OR SO

I've been making this pasta salad for twenty-five years. I first had it at my friend Gena's house when she hosted me for a fun weekend in the Dallas area. It is a fan favorite, gang! Although it requires some chopping, it's easy to make with familiar ingredients, perfect for pot-lucks, picnics, grill-outs, and gatherings of all kinds. Teenagers love it especially so. Package it in airtight deli containers and give it with store-bought garlic knots and something sweet for a thoughtful and light meal. When in doubt, friends, make more than you think you'll need because folks come back bowl after bowl.

1 (12-ounce) box of garden rotini pasta

1 (6-ounce) can black olives, drained, then halved

1 1/2 cups cherry or grape tomatoes, halved

1 large yellow or orange bell pepper, finely chopped

1/2 green bell pepper, finely chopped

1/4 cup red onion, finely chopped

2 (5-ounce) packages turkey pepperoni, quartered

1 to 2 cups shredded Monterey Jack or Cheddar Jack cheese

Basil, cilantro, or parsley for garnish

1/3 cup mayonnaise
3/4 cup bottled zesty Italian dressing
1/2 teaspoon salt
1/2 teaspoon pepper
1/2 teaspoon granulated garlic
1/2 teaspoon dried oregano
1/4 teaspoon red pepper flakes

Bring the pasta water to a boil, season generously with salt, then boil the pasta according to package directions. Don't overcook it! It should have a little bite. Drain in a colander or fine mesh strainer, then run under cold water until cool.

While the pasta is boiling, whisk together all the ingredients for the dressing. Once the pasta has cooled off, transfer to your biggest serving or mixing bowl. Add the olives, tomatoes, bell peppers, onion, and pepperoni. Stir in the dressing and fold it all together. Then stir in the shredded cheese. Sample a bite and add more salt and pepper if needed.

Refrigerate for about 15 minutes, stir, and serve! Garnish each serving with basil, cilantro, or parsley if you'd like.

notes

- Turkey pepperoni performs entirely better than regular pepperoni in this recipe.
- I often double the dressing recipe because some may like their

pasta salad saucier. It also serves to freshen up the pasta salad if it needs to sit in the fridge for a while or even overnight.

♥ If you know that the pasta salad is going to be refrigerated for a while or overnight, then wait to add the shredded cheese until time to serve it.

CHAPTER 7

jesus: the multiplier

*O*f all the hospitality occasions that Jesus initiated or engaged in, the one we will look at in this chapter is the grandest of all. This assembly boasts the greatest number of people, the greatest amount of food, and maybe the most astonishing miracle up to this point in the Savior's ministry. It's a familiar story to many. It has been woven into the narrative of our culture as a regularly used reference or metaphor in conversation and in storytelling. Whether you've been in church your whole life or you've never stepped foot inside one, you're likely acquainted with this famous picnic.

Jesus fed the five thousand. This miracle is recorded across all four Gospel accounts in the Bible. The Gospels are the first four books of the New Testament, written by four of Jesus' disciples and friends. They are God-inspired accounts, from the Gospel writers' points of view, on much of the life of Christ. And in the case of the feeding of the five thousand, the Gospel writers reported different perspectives and details according to what they experienced that day. For example, Mark revealed the depth and heart of Jesus as he described the level of compassion Jesus had on the crowds, referring to them as "sheep without a shepherd" (Mark 6:34). In Luke's account, he named the location of the miracle, Bethsaida (Luke 9:10). John is the one who told us the origin of the food by saying, "Here is a boy with five small barley loaves and two small fish" (John 6:9). It was John who also mentioned the crowd's reaction as the miracle took place, reporting that the people were amazed, declaring, "Surely this is the Prophet who is to come into the world" (v. 14).

We, too, have marveled at the happenings on that hillside, the bottomless basket of fish, and the sheer number of folks who were fed. But when Jesus fed a crowd of five-thousand-plus that late afternoon, it spoke more about the Man than the meal itself. Take a look at Matthew's account of this event:

When Jesus heard what had happened, he withdrew by boat privately to a solitary place. Hearing of this, the crowds followed him on foot from the towns. When Jesus landed and saw a large crowd, he had compassion on them and healed their sick.

As evening approached, the disciples came to him and said, "This is a remote place, and it's already getting late. Send the crowds away, so they can go to the villages and buy themselves some food."

Jesus replied, "They do not need to go away. You give them something to eat."

"We have here only five loaves of bread and two fish," they answered.

"Bring them here to me," he said. And he directed the people to sit down on the grass. Taking the five loaves and the two fish and looking up to heaven, he gave thanks and broke the loaves.

Then he gave them to the disciples, and the disciples gave them to the people. They all ate and were satisfied, and the disciples picked up twelve basketfuls of broken pieces that were left over. The number of those who ate was about five thousand men, besides women and children." (Matthew 14:13–21)

We see right away that Jesus was retreating to a solitary place upon hearing some bad news. Christ had just learned that His cousin, ministry partner, and friend John the Baptist had been executed while in prison. So not only had Jesus received heartbreaking news, but He was well into His ministry life and, frankly, needed rest. He needed a break from being needed. Have you ever felt that way? Have you ever locked yourself in a bathroom to secure one minute of solace from people who were pulling on you at all times? Can you imagine how it felt to be Jesus? Always being needed, always teaching, always on call, always pouring Himself out for others?

Because of His humanity, Jesus was physically and emotionally fatigued. But upon arriving at His place of retreat, he saw that the crowds had followed and already gathered nearby. Matthew told us a lot about this crowd. They were sick, needy, desperate, hungry, and wanting time with the Lord.

When Jesus saw the crowd, He had compassion on them. His heart was stirred. The One who was brokenhearted still found room in His heart for others. Jesus, who was seeking to get away, still found a way to extend a welcome. Even though Christ Himself was in a time of need, He still recognized and responded to the needs of others. And as we see in Matthew 14:23, His rest would come; it would just be delayed.

Moved by empathy, Jesus healed the sick of their ailments and diseases. He taught them truth and shared wisdom from the

Scriptures. And y'all, this wasn't a roomful of folks; this was a crowd. Thousands had gathered for as far as the eye could see, which meant long lines, wait times, and logistical issues. But Jesus kept at it, ministering to them one by one, listening, healing, making relational connections, loving them well into the day. With the lines and the level of needs, the disciples realized that this whole thing could go into the night. They likely took delight at the first 837 people Jesus had welcomed and engaged with. But now, they decided it was time to break up the party. And they had already prepared their list of reasons.

So, interrupting Jesus, the disciples explained the current situation and forecasted the circumstance that would surely lie ahead. Across the Gospel accounts, we see the disciples come up with a variety of objections for Jesus to consider. And while I don't believe they had any ill intent or mean-spiritedness, I do believe there was a little bit of bellyaching going on: *Well, look at the time, Lord! We have thousands of people here who haven't eaten in hours, and it'll be dark before we know it. We have no food, and it would cost a fortune for us to feed them. Why don't You let these good people go so they can run through McDonald's and feed their families on their way home?*

The disciples were known to have grumbled a time or two. And it was understandable in this case. Not only were they exhausted and grieving, but according to Matthew 14:12, they had also picked up John the Baptist's decapitated body from the prison and had performed the painstaking task of burying him. Then instead of the rest and solace they had set out to experience alongside Jesus, they spent the day with Him ministering to mobs of people with needs. Likewise, the disciples were probably protective of Christ, their friend and teacher, whom they knew was depleted as well. So they communicated a list of reasons why they weren't interested in any kind of mass-showing of hospitality, why they were done ministering to folks for the day.

> *This is the wrong place.*
> *It's not the best time.*
> *What we have isn't good enough.*
> *This place isn't gonna do.*
> *We don't have to be the ones to feed them.*
> *There are plenty of other places they can go to have their*
> *needs met.*
> *Feeding these people would be too expensive.*
> *We don't have the right resources.*
> *There are significant supply chain issues.*
> *My living room isn't big enough.*
> *I had such a long week at the office.*
> *I'm not even a good cook.*

Okay, the disciples may not have launched those last few objections, but I know some of us have. But look how Jesus replied: "They do not need to go away. You give them something to eat" (v. 16). Jesus didn't turn away the crowds, and in a surprise turn of events, He gave the disciples an assignment: you feed them.

You feed them. That is *so* Jesus of Him! Peter and the disciples will hear something very similar from Him around the fish fry in the coming months, remember that? This event is a purposeful sneak peek at what is to come.

So the disciples, in the first-ever case of crowdsourcing, took inventory and found a young boy who had brought his lunch that day and offered to share it. And the disciples brought it to Jesus. *Okay, so, Jesus, we set up a GoFundMe, and what was given was only enough to cover five small loaves of bread and two fish.* They knew what they had gotten their hands on was not enough to make a dent in the depth of hunger represented in the crowd. But Jesus said, "Bring them here to me" (v. 18).

Jesus took the food, lifted His eyes toward heaven, and prayed. I can't help but consider the Lord's Prayer in Matthew 6:11: "Give us today our daily bread." I can't help but think about Moses, who had a crowd of two million to feed in Exodus 16. He called upon God, who rained down bread from heaven! I can't help but recall Elisha, who was given only twenty loaves to feed his crowd of starving soldiers in the midst of a famine in the book of 2 Kings. His servant even questioned it: "How can I set this before a hundred men?" (4:43). But Elisha trusted in the provision of God, who had promised there would be plenty of food to feed the men with leftovers to spare!

So understanding what had been done and what He was about to do, Jesus prayed. Then He considered the logistics, divided everyone into smaller groups on the grass, and turned the neon sign to Open. Jesus became the kitchen, and His disciples became the waitstaff. Jesus became the manufacturer, and He designated the disciples as distributors. Can you imagine this scene? Groups of fifty in clusters around the countryside to create a manageable distribution system!

And think about this: the Bible says there were about five thousand *men*. The men were counted, but these men likely had spouses and maybe even the average of 2.25 children, which would equal closer to twenty thousand bodies and bellies there that day! Feeding five thousand people would be a feat, but feeding twenty thousand is truly unimaginable. That's larger than the capacity of most college basketball arenas. It's double the population of the little Arkansas town I grew up in!

Now contemplate what the process actually entailed as the disciples delivered the food to the groups of fifty. Go to Jesus, get a basketful of food, deliver to the people. Return to Jesus, get a basketful of food, deliver to the people. Walk *back* to Jesus, get a basketful, and take to the people.

Now there's a word problem I am not skilled enough to calculate. I have other gifts. However, my husband, Dr. Sam Hannon, is unquestionably skilled with numbers. So according to Sam's calculations, twelve disciples delivering food to twenty thousand folks who sat in groups of fifty would equal four hundred total trips! Further calculations show that each disciple would have made thirty-three trips back and forth between Jesus and the crowd. And we're operating under the assumption here that each trip held enough to feed the entire circle of fifty; the number of trips could easily be doubled depending on how much food the disciples could carry or if anyone wanted seconds.

Imagine how the expressions on their faces and their gaits must've changed as they played a role in what was happening. Their first food delivery may have been half-hearted and listless. They were exhausted and felt like they had nothing to give. (Raise your hand if you've shown hospitality from this posture! *Me!*) But in obedience to do the work put before them, as they returned to Jesus over and over, witnessing the hand of God, I bet they picked up the pace, almost running in awe and delight! Were they giddy in amazement? Did their weariness fade with the wonder of the work? Did they pass one another in their comings and goings with wide-eyed joy?

How many trips back and forth did the disciples take before they realized that Jesus was more than enough? They certainly didn't have the resources to pull off the task before them. Did they ever think He would run out of food? At what point did they make the connection that as long as they kept returning to Christ, there would always be something to give?

I wonder how long it took the disciples to realize that Jesus is the one who satisfies. As these men kept serving the goodness of God to people, when did it click? They had seen Jesus satisfy the crowd's physical needs, healing them, teaching them, and now feeding them. But when did they fully recognize that He was the one who could satisfy not only the body but the soul?

I wonder at what point in their back-and-forthing they understood that Jesus was the Source. I wonder when they comprehended that Jesus was using this opportunity not only to benefit the physical needs of folks who were there, but He was also revealing to His disciples that this is the way life and ministry works—we must go to Him before we go to them.

The story concludes that the multitudes were not only fed but they were filled. And Scripture tells us that there were leftovers (Matthew 14:20)! Because won't He do it, y'all? Baskets upon baskets upon baskets filled with food, when they started with only one.

♥ ♥ ♥

There is so much to consider when exploring the miracle of Christ feeding the masses. So many things worth examining for our own hospitality and ministry lives:

How the crowd sought to be near Jesus out of curious faith.
How Christ considered the needs of others more important
    than His own needs at a time when He had set out to rest.
How the disciples grumbled and offered all kinds of reasons
    not to initiate a hospitality event with the crowd, but they
    served out of obedience anyway.
How the disciples' willingness to serve out of nothing resulted
    in plenty.

How the young boy offered what he had to the Lord.

How Christ turned soup things into spiritual things, as He's
known to do.

Although the cast of characters in this story has so much to
teach us, we can't help but look at Jesus; after all, the miracle isn't
the main course—He is. In this narrative of nourishment, Jesus is
the one who multiplies, He is the one who satisfies, and He is the
source who supplies.

The kindness and innocence of the young boy to offer his sack
lunch for the sake of the cause is noteworthy. He had in his posses-
sion an everyday, basic meal—a modern-day PBJ. It was nothing
special, certainly not hardy or gourmet. But he offered it to Jesus in
obedience and faith, resulting in a hospitality event of epic propor-
tions! Why? Because Jesus is the one who multiplies. He encourages
us to bring Him all that we have, however big or small, and watch
Him bless it, multiplying it for His glory in our lives *and* in the lives
of others. He turns our miniscule into something magnificent! He
takes our sack lunches and multiplies them into the kind of abundance that impacts the lives of those around us. What we consider
not to be enough becomes bottomless when we hand it over to the
power of the Lord God.

Not only was every person served that day in a spectacular
distribution display, but the Bible tells us, "They all ate and *were
satisfied*" (Matthew 14:20). You would never expect the Lord Jesus
to offer only bites or morsels of food to the hungry crowd, leaving
them wanting for more. No, this meal that Christ served was sub-
stantial enough that the Bible says they were satisfied. By doing so,
Jesus revealed that He is more than enough! Jesus is the one who
satisfies. The nourishment He provides fills body *and* soul alike.
Christ declared about Himself in John 6:35, "I am the bread of life.

Whoever comes to me will never go hungry, and whoever believes in me will never be thirsty."

What started as little bites became a lavish bounty revealing Jesus is the one who *multiplies*. What Christ put forth in order to meet the needs of body and soul abundantly revealed He is the one who *satisfies*. And as the disciples traipsed back and forth from baskets to bellies, they kept returning to Jesus, revealing that He is also the source who *supplies*. He was the source where they'd be replenished. He was the source where they'd catch their breaths and be restored. He was the source who filled their hands. He was the one who fortified their hearts. He was the source that enabled, encouraged, and empowered them to deliver good things into the lives of those around them.

This monumental meal served not only to meet physical needs in a grand display of the Lord's power and divine nature, but it also served as a purposeful practicum for the disciples. The Lord Jesus in the most providential way allowed His disciples, including Peter, to participate in this miracle meal on the hillside, ministering to the overwhelming crowds, in order to give them grounds for understanding the mission that would soon be shared on the shore.

Remember, Christ later told Peter, "Feed my sheep" (John 21:17). Jesus was saying, "You are now My chosen ambassadors, My deliverers of spiritual nourishment to the world. Although I'll no longer physically be with you, I'll always supply you with everything you need to do good works and to carry out the will of God in the lives of those around you. Just as you did in Bethsaida, keep returning to Me time and time again, for I am the source who will enable you, who will encourage you, who will empower you to go and feed My sheep."

♥ ♥ ♥

The vision that Christ cast for Peter and his friends is the same vision He has given to us, the church. As believers in Jesus Christ, we are commanded to be light and share hope, to recognize needs and to care for those around us, to make known the good news of the gospel. We're likewise reminded throughout God's Word of the importance of drawing strength from the Source. Our 1 Peter passage affirms this as well! Following the encouragement to love deeply, welcome gladly, and serve faithfully like the disciples on the hillside, note the source of our strength:

> Above all, love each other deeply, because love covers over a multitude of sins. Offer hospitality to one another without grumbling. Each of you should use whatever gift you have received to serve others, as faithful stewards of God's grace in its various forms. If anyone speaks, they should do so as one who speaks the very words of God. *If anyone serves, they should do so with the strength God provides*, so that in all things God may be praised through Jesus Christ. To him be the glory and the power for ever and ever. Amen. (4:8–11)

Did you see it? Peter took the lesson he learned on the hillside and shared it with the rest of us. When we minister to others, we serve not from our own strength but from the strength God provides. We go to Him before we go to them. Jesus is the Source!

In John 15:5–8, Jesus said,

> I am the vine; you are the branches. If you remain in me and I in you, you will bear much fruit; apart from me you can do nothing. If you do not remain in me, you are like a branch that is thrown away and withers; such branches are picked up, thrown into the fire and burned. If you remain in me and my words remain in you,

ask whatever you wish, and it will be done for you. This is to my Father's glory, that you bear much fruit, showing yourselves to be my disciples.

This imagery emphasizes the value of the Source that is Christ Jesus our Lord. The health and fruitfulness of our spiritual lives are drawn from an abiding relationship with Him that ultimately flourishes, allowing us to be used for His glory. Apart from Him, we run out of steam, we drag our feet, we wither, and we have nothing truly satisfying to offer the world. Remaining in the vine nourishes, feeds, sustains, and allows us to flourish and thrive—in ministry, in hospitality, and in life.

♥ ♥ ♥

Our friends the Johnsons are perfect examples of what it looks like to draw from the Source in order to deliver the goodness of God into the lives of others. Royce and Susan are Northwest Arkansas friends who, both having been ophthalmic surgeons, retired early and became global workers in Kenya and the South of France before putting down roots in Northern Ireland. Royce and Susan serve in leadership at the C. S. Lewis Institute in Belfast. And Sam and I have had the privilege of partnering with them in ministry both at home and abroad.

Royce and Susan know what it means to abide. They go to the Source before they go to the people, believing that nothing good happens without Jesus' touch. Through faithful prayers, they go to the Source for wisdom, guidance, and direction. They pray for God's favor over people, families, worship services, and more. They ask God to give them the words to say, the wisdom to share, and the best way to meet others' needs. They pray for people who come in their door and for those same folks when they leave. They pray for their home, for their guests, for their hospitality, and for rest. They pray before they gather. They pray in order to give. They pray before a prayer meeting! They pray every time they belt up in a moving vehicle. I've even heard Susan mutter prayers over her curry while she stirs. They have given their lives to ministry and their home for biblical hospitality. And they minister to people faithfully out of an abundant life that returns to the Source time after time.

Jesus is the one who multiplies. Jesus is the one who satisfies. Jesus is the source who supplies all that we need to love, welcome, and serve.

♥ ♥ ♥

Food for Thought

- ♥ The miracle of Christ feeding the five thousand is full of principles for our lives. What impacted you the most in this narrative? What was your favorite moment? In what ways do you relate to the disciples?

- ♥ Why is it important to recognize that Jesus is the source of our ministry of hospitality? Why are we encouraged to return to Him before we go to the people? What happens when we don't abide in Him and instead serve others out of our own strength?

- ♥ What does Jesus bestow to us—with what does He fill our hearts and our hands—that allows us to minister to those around us?

- ♥ What are some practical ways we can go to Him before we go to them?

dutch oven artisan bread

MAKES ONE ROUND BOULE

Jesus multiplied bread on the hillside to feed thousands. He broke bread with His disciples at the Last Supper. And He cooked fish and bread on the shore with Peter. So I figured it was fitting to share a doable bread recipe with y'all here! This recipe requires a cast-iron Dutch oven and more steps than my usual recipes. But it's so worth it! Jesus is the one who satisfies our souls, but this bread will make your belly very happy.

2 tablespoons of fresh yeast (not instant and not old!)
2 tablespoons sugar
2 cups very warm water (think baby-bottle warm)
4 to 4 1/2 cups bread flour, divided
1 1/2 tablespoons salt

In the bowl of a stand mixer fitted with the dough hook, use a hand whisk to gently whisk together the yeast, sugar, and very warm water. Let it proof for 10 minutes without stirring until it grows, gets foamy, and smells like heaven.

In a separate bowl, mix 3 cups of the flour with the salt.

With the mixer on low, add the flour mixture one cup at a time to the yeast mixture until you have added all three cups, mixing to combine with each cup. The dough will start to come together but will still be sticky. Add the rest of the flour in 1/2-cup increments until the dough completely comes together in a ball. It may not take all of the flour.

Let the mixer knead the dough for a few minutes. Then dump the dough onto a lightly floured counter and continue to knead for about five minutes or until the dough is smooth. (Search a "how to knead bread" video online so you're sure to do it correctly!) You may want to sprinkle the top of the dough with a little flour to make it easier to handle.

Place the dough in a large bowl brushed lightly with vegetable oil and cover the top with a slightly damp kitchen towel. Let it rise for 20 to 30 minutes in a draft-free place and preferably a place where it's warmer. I usually place mine on top of my stove.

Preheat the oven to 400ºF *with the cast-iron Dutch oven inside.*

Remove the towel from the bowl and *carefully* remove the ball of dough. Do *not* punch down the dough as you would in other recipes. Lightly coat both the bottom and top of the dough with flour. *Carefully* remove the preheated Dutch oven and just as *carefully* drop the dough in the center of the preheated Dutch oven. Cut a crisscross of slits in the top of the loaf with the tip of a sharp knife, only about 1/4-inch deep, which will give your loaf a beautiful artisan appearance.

Bake in the oven for 30 minutes with the lid *on*, then remove the lid and bake for another 7 to 10 minutes until the top is golden and crusty.

Remove the bread from the Dutch oven onto a wood board and let it cool slightly before cutting with a serrated bread knife. I love this bread served with salted butter and honey or dragged through good-quality olive oil!

CHAPTER 8

jesus: the magnified

*W*e began our time together considering the biblical command given to us by Paul to "practice hospitality" (Romans 12:13). We explored a heartening and proven approach, demonstrated by the early church, that allows us to share our lives, resources, and the hope of heaven with those around us. That puts on full display our sincere love of God and devotion to others. That demonstrates our zeal and fervor, our joy and faithfulness, and the fullness of life in Christ. We've observed Jesus' hospitality ministry, when He gathered folks in homes, around tables, on the shore, and in fields—when He was often the guest, sometimes the host, and even the cook. We've spent much of our time exploring the practical encouragement for hospitality found in 1 Peter 4:8–11. We love deeply, welcome gladly, and serve faithfully, drawing strength to serve from the Source who provides.

But why do we do all of this? Why do we love, welcome, and serve? Well, the purpose of a life given to hospitality is found in the final part of our 1 Peter 4:8–11 passage. Let's go there one last time! *blows party horn*

> Above all, love each other deeply, because love covers over a multitude of sins. Offer hospitality to one another without grumbling. Each of you should use whatever gift you have received to serve others, as faithful stewards of God's grace in its various forms. If anyone speaks, they should do so as one who speaks the very words of God. If anyone serves, they should do so with the strength God provides, *so that in all things God may be praised through Jesus Christ.* To him be the glory and the power for ever and ever. Amen.

Our beloved passage (that I hope the Lord has tattooed on your heart) declares that we love, welcome, and serve *so that* in all things God may be praised through Jesus Christ. The words "so that" point to the purpose and end goal. There's a rhyme and reason. We embrace a lifestyle of everyday biblical hospitality so that God receives the praise and the glory!

We don't love people deeply in order to get thank-you notes or social media shout-outs or to put a spiritual feather in our caps. We don't welcome people gladly so that we'll hear compliments on the flowers or rave reviews about the food. We don't serve people faithfully so that they'll be gratefully indebted or hold us in high regard for our selflessness and humility. (See how that actually *doesn't* work?) We don't engage in biblical hospitality so that *we* receive accolades. For followers of Christ, our hope is to make *His name* famous, not our own.

What does it mean to make His name famous? To give God

glory? It means that we want to honor Him, to please Him, to reflect Him so that others look beyond us and see Him instead. Allowing God to receive the praise shows that we understand there is a greater purpose and a higher aim. Hospitality that glorifies God not only savors the people and the warm feelings of the moment but also seizes that moment to make His heart known.

When speaking at a Campus Outreach staff conference, John Piper said this about living to glorify the Lord: " 'Glorifying' means feeling and thinking and acting in ways that reflect his greatness, that make much of God, that give evidence of the supreme greatness of all his attributes and the all-satisfying beauty of his manifold perfections."[1]

Glorifying God is a grand assignment! Feeling and thinking and acting in ways that reflect the immeasurable magnitude of almighty God seems like a lofty goal. Glorifying God may sound like a grander assignment than our little lives can offer. I mean, "[giving] evidence of the supreme greatness of all [God's] attributes" is a tall order for a housewife, teacher, introvert, widow, young mom, or whatever describes your life right now. We often think that people whose lives bring glory to God are doing the big things like going to the farthest places, speaking to the biggest crowds, releasing bestsellers, and posting super engaging content on social media, but we glorify God in the small things too. The Bible tells us that "all things" can give Christ glory. And 1 Corinthians 10:31 says it as well: "So whether you eat or drink or whatever you do, do it all for the glory of God." *All.* Do you see that? *All* we do is *all* for Him. The big things, the small things, and everything in between can make much of God when the goal is for Him to receive glory!

Considering our call to give God praise through the ministry of hospitality, "all things" includes the everyday things! When we roll out a pie crust, run the vacuum over the floor, or box up an extra portion for someone across town. When we host our small group or make burgers for our student ministry. When we invite another mom to bring her kids over for Popsicles in the backyard. When we text a friend and drop off a store-bought blueberry bread. When we peel shrimp, swish a toilet, or pull up an extra chair. Whenever we choose to be intentional with our kitchening! Having a deeper heart and a more meaningful agenda than just filling bellies and hugging necks allows the One we serve to be recognized and esteemed. Our higher hospitality cultivates holy ground.

What makes a place holy ground? In Exodus 3, Moses had an encounter with the Lord where he was told the ground upon which he stood was holy, because it was at that very location where God chose to reveal Himself in a real and powerful way. God indicates all throughout Scripture His great desire to reveal Himself, not just to Moses but to the hearts of men and women. Through creation, through circumstances, through His people, through His Word, and in the person of Jesus Christ, God reveals Himself over and over so that each one would know Him!

He reveals that He is both personal and powerful.
He reveals that He is all-knowing with boundless wisdom.
He reveals that He is sovereign and trustworthy.
He reveals His holiness, perfectly complete.
He shows that He is true, righteous, and just.
He shows that He is loving, merciful, and full of grace.
He proves that He is faithful and never changes.
He makes known His heart and His will in the lives of men and women.

Fueled by this same desire to make Himself known to the hearts of humanity, God takes our open homes and open hearts and transforms them into holy ground. He makes small things significant things. He transforms our everyday things into eternal things. He meets us at the table so that others can taste and see that He is good (Psalm 34:8)!

Think about it: if a place where God chooses to reveal His heart and His nature to people is deemed divine, then your kitchen counter, your patio, or even the rug in your playroom can be considered "holy ground" when they're surrendered to the Lord God, offered as a platform for His glory to be revealed in great and mighty ways! Your home could be the place where someone senses something spiritual for the first time. Your kitchen table could be the place where God reveals His grace and forgiveness in your neighbor's life. Your living room could be the place where a grieving friend feels the Lord's comfort and peace. Your porch swing could be a sacred place where God reveals profound truth through prayer. Wherever this kind of eternal encounter happens for God's glory, you'll find yourself in a place set apart. You're standing on holy ground.

And remember, people who encounter God have lives that will never be the same.

My hope is that we will be people who love deeply, welcome gladly, and serve faithfully, and that we will share God's heart with the world through everyday hospitality.

After all, God takes small things and makes them significant things. He turns soup things into spiritual things. All we have to do is open our homes, invite people in, and ask Him to.

Food for Thought

♥ What are we tempted to desire for ourselves when we extend hospitality? What are you most guilty of selfishly seeking? Be transparent with this: A thank-you? Approval? Applause?

- ♥ What does 1 Peter 4:11 tell us should be the ultimate purpose of biblical hospitality? Why do we love deeply, welcome gladly, and serve faithfully?
- ♥ What does it mean to glorify God, to bring Him praise? Does that charge on your life intimidate you? How can your everyday hospitality glorify God?
- ♥ Can you think of a place that for you is "holy ground"? Is there a place where God has shown up, revealed Himself, and met you in a real and personal way? How can your home become holy ground for someone else? Oh, dear ones, pray that He will use your home as holy ground!

♥ ♥ ♥

sour cream blueberry streusel muffins

MAKES 12 MUFFINS

These blueberry streusel muffins are a friend favorite, family favorite, and fan favorite for sure! They are sweet and tender, crumbly and crunchy. Package them up for a friend who could use a dose of thoughtfulness. Have a batch or two available for weekend company, holidays, and more. They're delicious for breakfast, a snack, dessert, or to satisfy a late-night sweet tooth! It's just the right recipe to make and share if you find yourself with a bunch of extra blueberries.

1 $\frac{1}{2}$ cups all-purpose flour

$\frac{3}{4}$ cup sugar

$\frac{1}{2}$ teaspoon salt

2 teaspoons baking powder

$\frac{1}{3}$ cup vegetable oil

$\frac{1}{3}$ cup milk

1 large egg, room temperature

1 teaspoon vanilla

$\frac{1}{3}$ cup sour cream

1 cup fresh blueberries

-FOR THE TOPPING-

½ **cup sugar**

⅓ **cup all-purpose flour**

1 ½ **teaspoons ground cinnamon**

⅛ **teaspoon salt**

¼ **cup unsalted butter, cubed and soft**

Preheat the oven to 400°F. Line a standard muffin tin with 12 paper muffin cups.

To make the streusel topping, mix together all the ingredients for the topping, mashing and incorporating with a dinner fork or pastry cutter; set aside.

For muffins, whisk together the flour, sugar, salt, and baking powder in a large mixing bowl. Make a well in the middle of the dry ingredients, and stir in oil, milk, and egg. Add vanilla and sour cream. Stir with a wooden spoon. Fold in blueberries gently without busting them.

Using an ice cream scoop with a release lever, fill muffin cups about ⅔ full and pile the crumb topping on the tops. Heap it on!

Bake for 20 minutes, then check them in one-minute intervals until they're done. Don't overbake them. Cool muffins completely in the pan or the tops will separate from the bottoms. Gently run a knife around the edges and carefully lift out of the tin. Replace any crumbly streusel topping that falls off. Or eat it. (I prefer the latter.) Serve with salted butter.

gather & give: a hospitality handbook

*I*n this book, we've explored the hospitality ministry of Jesus—the ones to whom He extended an invitation, the ones He gathered, and the breadth of spiritual food He dished out when He got them in homes or around a meal. We see His initiative to assemble people around a table, where He accomplished significant heart-work, sharing truth, redemption, grace, and love.

Likewise, we've come to understand how God's love in us *for others* inspires our invitation, allowing us to serve them the way Christ served us. And we've seen that by embracing a lifestyle of everyday hospitality, we open up opportunities to be Jesus, to shine light in the darkness, and to share God's heart with the world.

As I wrote the words of this book, I walked and prayed, wrote and prayed, worshiped and prayed that the Lord God would stir your hearts to hospitality. My hope in the Lord is that you will recognize people's value, see their needs, invite them into your lives, welcome them into your homes, get them together around a shared meal, and let loose the Spirit of God to do what He purposes *through* you *in* them!

I hope you're on board. But you may be wondering, *Where do I begin?* And that, my friends, is where this handbook comes in. I would never dream of leaving you hanging without loads of encouragement and application for how to get the hospitality ball rolling. So this hospitality handbook is intended to be a spur in your side, a lightbulb over your head, and gas in your tank to love, welcome, and serve.

Now, magazine-worthy hospitality tips are superfluous, so I don't plan to include any of those here. While I do have great appreciation for all the bells and whistles, that level of welcome is reserved for special occasions in order to create a fond memory. This book isn't about event-driven hospitality—it's about *everyday* hospitality. So we are about to go basic. My goal is to uncomplicate the effort; to position your home to love, welcome, and serve; and to provide simple ways to fulfill this missional command.

There are two approaches to extending everyday hospitality, and they're so simple! These two ideas aren't earth-shattering or mind-blowing. The heavens aren't going to part, because hospitality isn't quantum physics, y'all. Ready? There are two approaches to hospitality: gathering and giving.

♥ ♥ ♥

Gathering was the strategy of the early church in Acts 2:46. You may have this verse on a chalkboard or a dish towel in your home. It says, "They broke bread in their homes and ate together with glad and sincere hearts." We see in the book of Acts that ministry and fellowship for the glory of God happened when folks gathered together in homes!

Likewise, we open the door and invite people into our homes to share warmth, grace, and nourishment in their lives. We hug in the entry, hang out in the kitchen, and hold court at the table, lingering and laughing around empty plates of food. We ask questions, go deeper, and camp out on our commonality. It can be a pretty meal with a memorable atmosphere, or it can be an impromptu gathering over casual food or takeout. It can be a neighbor or two, a tableful of eight, or a crowd standing shoulder to shoulder eating street tacos on paper plates. Sometimes the piles are picked up, the candles are lit, and the music is playing. Other times there are shoes in the living room, Goldfish crackers under the coffee table, and plastic cups filled with store-bought tea.

No matter the gathering, the intention is to build community and to share with others the grace and goodness you have received from God. It's that easy. I love this quote by Jean Brillat-Savarin in his book *The Physiology of Taste*: "To invite people to dine with us is to make ourselves responsible for their well-being for as long as they're under our roofs."[1] Isn't that so good? What a privilege it is to be able to use your home, your gifts, and the comfort of a shared meal to take charge of people's happiness for as long as you're with them by the power of the Holy Spirit in you! In Hebrews 10:24–25, we're encouraged not to give up gathering together but to meet with a spirit of sincerity, providing connection to one another, offering hope to one another, spurring one another on toward love and good deeds, and drawing near to one another and to God. Gosh, that's good stuff!

In her book *Bread and Wine: A Love Letter to Life Around the Table*, Shauna Niequist said, "Gather the people you love around your table and feed them with love and honesty and creativity. Feed them with your hands and the flavors and smells that remind you of home and beauty and the best stories you've ever heard, the best stories you've ever lived."[2] Gather them, feed them, nourish their souls. Shedding the expectations and misconceptions about gathering in order to get to the heart of hospitality helps us all realize that we can do this. We can embrace everyday hospitality in order for God to change lives. We just open our doors, invite people in, and ask Him to.

♥ ♥ ♥

We know from Acts 2 that the early church not only gathered together but they also demonstrated hospitality by sharing all that they had with one another and those who were in need. Although gathering is primarily what comes to mind when we consider hospitality, the act of giving food and sharing with others is another expression of hospitality. Sometimes the situation doesn't allow for folks to come to us and meet us in our homes in order to minister to them. The greater heart-impact may be made by sending food, meeting on their turf for a meal, or showing up with food.

Unlike gathering, which involves inviting people into our homes, the act of giving food exports our hearts to someone else's. Giving food and sharing what we have with others communicates that they are seen, heard, and considered. It speaks to others when they're hurting that we hurt with them. It says, "You are not alone." When we share food with others, it's kind, merciful, and compassionate, as the psalmist described the character of God time and time again. It demonstrates His heart to provide, to nourish, to sustain.

Sharing food with people around us can be done in a wide variety of ways and on a variety of levels. And it isn't only compassionate and kind—giving food can be uniquely creative! Delivering care in the form of a compassion meal. Hearing of a need and responding with comfort food. Showing up with soup or a casserole in a crisis. (Oh, the power of a casserole in a crisis!) Online food delivery and mail-order meals that extend our reach.

Giving food is using a pound cake to say "thank you" or "I'm celebrating with you." It's delivering a quick bread to say "I appreciate who you are and what you do." It can be entirely homemade, halfway homemade, or even a big fountain drink with the good ice and a red straw. Whatever the reason and whatever the fare, giving food reminds others that God is the giver of all good things.

♥ ♥ ♥

As I've examined my own hospitality journey, I've realized that one of the greatest reasons I was hesitant to host or, regrettably, let opportunities to share food pass by, is that I was unprepared. I felt vulnerable and utterly caught off guard. I didn't have a plan of any kind whatsoever. I was unschooled in the hows and whats of everyday hospitality. But my heart *did desire to* use my home, my greatest and most natural platform, to love people well.

What I have come to understand is that my preparation affects my invitation. This all sounds vaguely familiar, doesn't it? Remember when we examined what it means to serve and saw how Titus 3:1 and Hebrews 10:24–25 encouraged believers to be *ready* to do good works? And recall how the idea of readiness is fundamental to someone showing generosity? Readiness affects our willingness to welcome and our availability to serve.

So in the spirit of readiness, I'm about to get super practical with suggestions, supplies, and personal lessons learned to help prepare your home for hospitality.[3]

♥ ♥ ♥

gather

WHO IS WORTHY OF OUR WELCOME?

New friends, old friends, family, and neighbors
Your kids' friends and your kids' friends' families
The churched and unchurched
Business associates, coworkers, employees, and staff
Church, community, and civil leaders
The never-married, divorced, widows, and widowers
Those displaced by disaster—natural, relational, or other
College students, international students, missionaries, and
    others who ache for home
Whoever the Lord puts on your heart

GENERAL GATHERING SUPPLIES TO KEEP STOCKED

Bulk paper products like plates, bowls, cups, napkins, and
    plastic utensils
Foil pans for big-batch cooking and easy cleanup
Gallon pitchers, lemonade mix, tea bags, and plenty of sugar,
    y'all
Restaurant and deli-style takeout containers for sending home
    leftover portions
Sturdy, dishwasher-safe dinnerware, glasses, and flatware for
    quicker cleanup

GENERAL GATHERING TIPS

♥ Shop your big-box store or restaurant supply stores for takeout containers. Keep a variety!

♥ Keep pretty, seasonal paper napkins to put with plain dinner plates or disposable plates.

♥ Buy a flat of inexpensive white glass votive candles to burn. Lighting two or three votives on a table is cozy but still casual.

♥ Remove any big centerpiece off your table. The hope is to see faces, not flowers!

♥ On the flipside of formal centerpieces, buy inexpensive grocery store flowers. Trim them and put them in whatever container you have on hand—glass jars, pitchers, vases, aluminum cans, little glass bottles. I save all kinds of containers, cans, bottles, and more to repurpose for my super affordable blooms! I stick them in bathrooms, on nightstands, and beyond!

♥ Keep a tub of disinfectant wipes under each bathroom sink for easy and quick cleaning.

♥ Play music! It's fun, fills the quiet, and is a conversation starter. Think Sinatra for pasta night, '80s hits for a gathering on the patio, or country music for a BBQ dinner.

♥ Your meal doesn't have to be ready to serve as soon as people walk in the door. Arrival times may vary, or there could be delays. Set out easy room-temperature bites like nuts, cheese, grapes, crackers, or chips and salsa for folks to nibble on. Then finish the rest of the meal when they arrive. Most people find it comforting and welcoming to see someone at work in their kitchen.

♥ When in doubt, put out a fix-your-own lineup like tacos, soups with toppings, or a loaded sandwich bar. This is especially helpful if you're concerned about how to fill the time. Plus it's hands-on and fun!

♥ If you are unsure of your cooking skills, then get takeout or grocery-store-prepared foods. Or order takeout for the main course, then toss together a salad and broil some bread. Remember, hospitality isn't entertaining. The focus of your gathering is not on you or your ability to wow people. You can minister to people with food, even if it isn't yours!

♥ Ask about food allergies your guests might have. Then do your best to honor those requests. The entire meal doesn't have to accommodate food allergies, but much can. And it's easier than you think!

♥ Learn to ask good questions. This is where loving people really manifests itself. Listen well, ask follow-up questions, then lean in with encouragement or gracious wisdom the Lord has shown you. But be sure your conversation is more about them than you.

♥ When guests leave, make notes about what you learned about them in your phone contacts: the names of their children, a reminder that they just lost a parent, or whether they prefer chocolate desserts to fruit desserts.

♥ Keep a note in your phone shared with your spouse, if you have one, where you list names of people you'd like to invite over. Jot notes and add names after seeing people at football games, the grocery store, out to dinner, or in the church foyer.

♥ Learn to laugh about things. If something goes wrong—you burn the bread or the pie doesn't set up—it's not the end of the world. Laugh about it! Your humanity is appealing; it makes them like you, because we've all burned the bread. (I did it two nights ago while writing this book.)

- ♥ Practice hospitality often! Practice is intended to make us better and more comfortable. And when you're comfortable offering hospitality, your joy will abound.
- ♥ Make hospitality a priority in your life, in your schedule, and in your family. Look ahead a month at a time, choose available times (weeknights, Sunday afternoons, etc.), and mark those dates for hospitality. Then extend invitations and use those nights to love and nourish others! Giving yourself plenty of time to plan and to be prepared will enhance your delight and lessen your stress.
- ♥ If you are early in your friendship with someone and a full meal feels like a step too far, then just invite them to run by for something simple, like bread pudding and decaf coffee on the patio one night.
- ♥ Offer a casual prayer over your guests either at dinner or just before they leave. We have become less likely to pray before we eat and more likely to pray over guests at the end of our time together. Sometimes both! But when the time is winding down and we stand up or even when we're already at the door, it's become our way to say, "Hey, can I pray for you really quick?" Then we pray briefly over what we've learned about our guests over the course of the gathering. We pray for jobs, sickness, biology tests, direction, protection over kids, upcoming weddings, houses to sell, and more.
- ♥ Pray before people arrive! Ask God to focus your heart on His purposes, not your performance. Call on the Lord to make known the fullness of life and love found in Christ Jesus. Pray that others will see what life in light of the gospel looks like. Pray that God's heart would be on glorious display in and through you.

TIPS FOR WHEN YOU'VE PLANNED TO HOST

In addition to the general gathering tips, here are some suggestions specific to the times when you have planned for hospitality.

- ♥ Keep things simple. Keep things simple. Keep things simple.
- ♥ Choose a menu that is proven and familiar, not complex or exasperating. This isn't the time to pull out a James Beard award-winning cookbook and try something lofty or new. Select a few recipes that can even be prepped a day or two before.
- ♥ The scheduling of guests affords the luxury of time and planning. Set times to pick up and clean, get groceries, make anything in advance, and get your bearings to lessen the frenzy.
- ♥ Prioritize what needs to be done, and be pragmatic about what doesn't.

TIPS FOR FEEDING LAST-MINUTE GUESTS

In addition to the general gathering tips, here are some suggestions regarding impromptu hospitality with short lead times and quick turnarounds.

- ♥ Keep things simple. Again, this is a universal, everyday hospitality truth.
- ♥ Have two or three quick and delicious recipes in your arsenal that incorporate shelf-stable ingredients you keep stocked. Then, if necessary, a quick trip to the nearest market for a

few fresh ingredients or produce will take just a few minutes. Grab the cilantro and lime or the box of spinach and a lemon, hit the self-checkout, and you're as good as gold!

♥ When in doubt, grab curbside takeout. Curbside pad Thai divvied around the table in your home is equally gracious and kind.

♥ Do a quick clean of the things that matter. Focus on the table where you'll be sitting and maybe the coffee table and end tables in the room where you may end up. Quickly run a vacuum cleaner over the rooms where you'll be. Spend thirty seconds in the bathroom of choice wiping the toilet and sink with your handy-dandy wipes under the sink. Tidy clutter. (Tidy clutter is better than cluttered clutter any day.) The rest, toss behind closed doors. The end. *No one is looking at the dust on your lampshades or ceiling fan blades.* Clean what matters and move on. An intense fifteen minutes of cleaning will do wonders. Whatever you've missed, point it out and laugh about it: "Oh look, there's a half-eaten sandwich under the table! Whose children are these anyway?"

♥ If you have a spouse or children, include your family members in the tidying and cleanup. Instilling the responsibility of helping show hospitality will give them a sense of ownership and, ultimately, shared joy!

♥ Remember, when you offer an impromptu invitation, your guests are aware that there's a short turnaround. Also remember that people rarely receive your invitation because they are dying to see your house or eat your food; they receive your invitation because they feel honored and valued, and they desire to spend time with *you*.

TIPS WHEN DINNER GUESTS ARE
OVERNIGHT COMPANY TOO

In addition to the general gathering tips, here are a few suggestions for when guests aren't just in your home for a meal, but they're staying overnight!

- ♥ If you have a designated guest room and guest bath, make sure it stays tidy and doesn't become a heated and cooled storage unit. Keep it picked up; you can always load the guest room closet with stuff, but keep the room ready so you'll be more likely to invite guests.

- ♥ If you do not have a designated guest room and your company will sleep in a family member's room, keep a set of neutral bedsheets in the closet just for guests. It's easier on you than having to wash and put on sheets. Plus it's likely a better night's sleep for your guests!

- ♥ Likewise, keep a reserved stack of bath towels, hand towels, and washcloths just for guests.

- ♥ Nab free toiletries and wrapped bars of soap when you're in a hotel! Keep them at the ready for guests to use when they're staying overnight in your home.

- ♥ Put a couple of bottled waters and a snack or two in their room for late-night munching, to eat between meals, or as road trip snacks when they leave.

- ♥ Don't plan an elaborate breakfast in the morning; instead, put out simple options, like yogurt, fruit, granola, muffins, or quick breads. People wake up and get around at different times of day, so a continental breakfast of sorts is entirely more approachable than a hot dish or short-order breakfast.

♥ Show guests how to use your coffee maker, if you have one, in the event they are earlier risers than you are. Tell them there's juice in the fridge they can pour as well. Set out a variety of drinking glasses and coffee mugs for them to use to kick-start their day!

TIPS FOR GATHERING TEENAGERS
AND COLLEGE STUDENTS

In addition to the general gathering tips, here are some suggestions specific to hosting teenagers and students. Easily our favorite and probably our best season of hospitality yet!

♥ Keep things simple. (Have you heard this before?)
♥ Teenagers are basically wild animals and college students are hungry and poor, so they have zero expectations and want only to be fed and nourished on every level. And if you have a comfy couch with blankets, you get bonus points in their hearts.
♥ Young people usually have vibrant, functioning metabolisms. So fancy, healthy, or fruit- and veggie-forward meals are not necessary.
♥ Young people often travel in herds, like deer. If you see one, then there are likely six others not far behind. So when hosting them, know that you will likely have more show up than you expected.
♥ On the flip side, students don't live by any semblance of a plan. So you may be counting on twelve kids for pizza, and three kids show up. It is what it is.
♥ Have an extra cell phone charger for them to use.

♥ Hosting teenagers requires you to be relaxed. Be relaxed about their scheduling or lack thereof, about some of your house rules, about noise, about things being just so, about messes, and about some of the things you might hear. I'm not saying they get to do whatever they want. I figure out gracious or funny ways to communicate some of my house preferences, like, "I'm so glad you're here! Would y'all mind kicking off your shoes at the door?" or, "Hey, would you mind eating that in the kitchen, because I don't trust your testosterone with that pork chop on my couches." But the majority of my preferences for order and tidiness go by the wayside in order to make them feel welcome. You may hear a crude word or off-color comment, and you will most definitely hear vulgar sounds. (They can't help it, y'all.) I let most of them go, because I'm in the business of building intentional relationships with kids so that they feel accepted and loved. You and I didn't have to clean ourselves up in order to enjoy a relationship with Jesus. So we should extend the same grace. A friend of mine wisely shared that adults need to learn the skill of being "breezy" in relation to the language and behavior of teenagers. In other words, don't freak out, don't be rigid, and don't overreact as we open our homes to students of all ages.

♥ Alternately, it's perfectly fine to rally the troops to throw away plates and help put things back together. As a matter of fact, their time with us should make them better human beings across the board. So encouraging them to hop up and do a clean sweep through the room is acceptable and wise! But it's all in the way you say it. Don't sound like a military general; be a gracious host who needs a little help!

♥ Serve recipes that can be easily scaled, like tacos, pastas, and soups.

♥ When in doubt, put out chips and salsa. Teens and young adults eat it at any time of day, whether they're hungry or not. And it doesn't matter if it even goes with whatever else you're serving. (Chicken fettuccine alfredo with chips and salsa? It's a thing.)

♥ Find out what their favorites are, and fix them sometime. Those college students will love you forever. It may not be their mom's recipe, but it'll surely taste like home.

♥ Teenagers and college students have mastered the art of showing up unannounced. And they're always hungry. So here's my list of shelf-stable items or ingredients with a long life that I always have in my pantry and fridge for when they come in the back door at 9:23 p.m. on a Saturday night:

  ♥ Chips and salsa or Velveeta cheese with Rotel tomatoes to make queso

  ♥ Microwave popcorn, peanut butter crackers, and a giant box of Goldfish crackers

  ♥ Flour tortillas, shredded cheese, refried beans or black beans for quick skillet quesadillas

  ♥ Frozen snacks like Bagel Bites, pizza rolls, frozen pizzas, crustless PBJs

  ♥ Saltine crackers, a block of cheddar cheese, summer sausage, yellow mustard, and jarred jalapeños for what we lovingly refer to as "Redneck Cheeseboard"

  ♥ Boxed brownies and quick cookie mixes that bake in thirty minutes or less

  ♥ Cereal, granola bars, power bars, pancake mix, and syrup, because one or eight of them will stay overnight

- For the nights that they end up staying overnight, keep a closet or cabinet full of blankets, comforters, quilts, and pillows. They'll learn to grab their favorites, and they'll learn to fold them and put them back when you've asked them kindly. Or they might throw them in the closet in a big wad. That counts in my book.
- Ask good (breezy) questions and give good (breezy) responses. Listen to them, hear them, and see them. Go in heavy with encouragement, and speak life into these young people. Lean in gently with grace and wisdom, truth and love, when the Lord nudges you at just the right time.
- Feed their bellies and love their hearts. And you'll establish a bond with them that'll last until they're grown.

♥ ♥ ♥

give

TO WHOM DO WE GIVE?

Friends who are moving closer, across town, or far away
New neighbors and families on your street
People who have cancer, job changes, or water damage
Those who have welcomed a life or lost one
Those in despair or darkness or disarray
Those celebrating a wedding or a big win
People you appreciate or are grateful for
People who are known by many or who most do not see

Folks who serve you, your family, your community, or your
  church
Those who need to be remembered or cared for
Whoever the Lord puts on your heart

GENERAL GIVING SUPPLIES TO KEEP STOCKED

♥ Bulk paper products for sending disposable plates, napkins,
  utensils for their convenience
♥ Foil pans and disposable serveware to eliminate cleanup and
  the need to return a pan
♥ Restaurant and deli-style takeout containers for packaging
  and portioning food
♥ Note cards and gift tags for including sentiments, Scripture
  verses, and instructions for baking and storing

GENERAL GIVING TIPS

♥ Some giving is planned, communicated, and scheduled via text
  or a meal plan, most often because of a birth or a death or
  other significant event. Be courteous and ask if the recipients
  would prefer for the meal to be dropped off at the door or if
  they'd prefer to hug necks. Extend an, "I am glad to do which-
  ever feels better to you right now!"
♥ Impromptu giving in order to celebrate with someone is fun!
  Surprise them at the door or at work with treats, their favorite
  coffee, etc. Send a text that lets them know you're running by
  to say hello and to cheer for them.

♥ Impromptu giving in order to grieve with someone is thoughtful but sensitive. Be sure to read the situation and get a sense of how you can serve them. Say something like, "I'd love to run by and bring you lunch" or, "Are you home where I can drop off a treat to lighten your heart?"

♥ Sometimes I leave a nonperishable food gift at someone's door or in their mailbox, then I send a text to let them know it's out there.

♥ Choose three meals that become your go-to giving meals— one homemade, one halfway homemade, and one delivery. For example, mine are chicken pot pie, curbside pulled pork sandwiches and beans with homemade banana pudding, and pizza delivery with breadsticks and salad, plus a sweet option and two-liter bottles of soda.

♥ As long as you're cooking a recipe for your family at home, double the recipe and cook two meals! Or if you're an empty nester, make a whole recipe for enchiladas but put half of it into a foil pan for someone else. I call that a "sharing batch." Then freeze it, if it's freezable. Or store it for a day or three in your fridge, because you will for sure hear of someone who would be blessed by it.

♥ When you have a perfectly good single or double serving left over on any given weeknight at home, package it in one of your stocked takeout containers to share with a single person, a young couple, an elderly couple, or a widow or widower.

♥ Be proactive and mindful when you are giving food. It's natural to give food in response to someone's situation, but you can also be thoughtful with food you have on hand, finding people to share it with. Giving food for no reason is considerate and kind.

♥ When you give food big or small for whatever reason, it's a delight if you're able to include a little gift or gift card too. Ideas include a dish towel, votive, lotion, or book. You can also give a gift card to a local market, bookstore, an online favorite, and more!

♥ Many people who've weathered grief, transition, or upheaval agree that one of the nicest and most practical hospitality efforts shown to them was having a load of grocery staples, paper goods, and toiletries brought to their house. That counts too!

♥ Sometimes it's effective to wait until the dust settles a little to offer to bring food—whether in tragedy, transition, or even in celebration. In the case of grief, loss, or a difficult situation, often there's a rush of help that their need long outlives.

♥ If sending food that requires assembling or preparing or has special storing and reheating instructions, be sure to include a note with instructions. Include your cell number with an invitation to text or call if they have questions.

♥ If you're sending food that is homemade and especially yummy or unique, source the recipe in a cookbook or blog or include a handwritten recipe card so they can make it for themselves in the future.

♥ Food delivery services available online and via apps are convenient for sending food to others, and it extends your reach beyond your own ability to drive or deliver yourself!

♥ When you order a meal for others via a food delivery app, consider letting them choose the restaurant and even submit their order to you so you're sure to get what they like. Remember to add the tip for the delivery driver and let your friends know you've taken care of it on their behalf!

♥ When in doubt, email a food delivery service gift card. It's instant, and they can use it when their need is greatest.

♥ A quick online search will turn up all kinds of gourmet frozen meals and treats that can be shipped. I love to send Williams-Sonoma chocolate croissants or frozen meal packages to friends and loved ones far away because I'm not close enough to cook for them myself. SpoonfulOfComfort.com is one of my favorites as well!

♥ Pray as you prepare, order, deliver, or drive food to the ones the Lord has put on your heart that He would comfort and cheer them. Ask God to use your efforts to remind them of His goodness and provision. Pray that they will taste and see that the Lord is good!

♥ ♥ ♥

Here we are, gang! You are locked and loaded with suggestions, encouragement, and some of the most practical tips for gathering and giving. I've shared plenty to prepare you to embrace everyday hospitality. I know you can do it! Remember to go to Jesus before you go to the people! The Lord God will give you all that you need to minister to those around you—to love His people well.

♥ ♥ ♥

Food for Thought

♥ What are the two primary expressions of a life given to hospitality? How have you experienced each of these in your life? Consider times when you've gathered others in your home or you've gathered with people in others' homes. Consider times when you savored hospitality through the giving or receiving of food. How did they make you feel?

♥ Identify your top three Gather tips. What are your top three

Giving tips? Do you have any tips to add? Can you think of practical ways to incorporate those into your life so that you are prepared to extend hospitality?

♥ Is the Lord stirring you to invite someone over or to initiate a hospitality encounter with someone in your life? Make a note in your phone or in these pages and take the necessary steps to make it happen. Pray along the way!

tales from the table

My own personal hospitality journey has been encouraged and for-tified by having been on both the giving and receiving end, and by observing the hospitality shown by others around me. And like you, I find such incredible inspiration to lean into this calling more and more as I hear stories of everyday hospitality demonstrated by those around me in the world. So what follows is a collection of real hos-pitality stories—stories of *Gather & Give* big and small, for every reason, in an array of creative and practical ways! My hope is that you will draw inspiration from these tales from the table, sensing a stirring to share God's heart through your own everyday hospitality.

♥ ♥ ♥

"My husband is a college baseball coach and I love to cook, so we have had three to four boys over every Wednesday night for the past two seasons, and we eat at our big wooden table my husband built, then play a game with them. It is the highlight of the week for my six- and nine-year-old daughters. Not only are we showing these boys what it looks like for their coach and leader to be a good father and husband, but we are showing our own kids how to minister and love on people who are in our circle and who God has placed in our lives for a reason."

—Emily in Clinton, MS

"My mom underwent surgery in 2008 to remove a cancerous tumor. The surgery was successful (my mom has been in remission since—praise God!), but my mom needed a recovery period, as expected. Even surviving cancer didn't stop her full-time job as a mom. I was eleven at the time, and my brother was fourteen. Our sweet neighbor met a need we didn't even make known and brought home-made chicken noodle soup and homemade apple pie to our doorstep. I was too young to understand the magnitude of that gesture, but I understand it now. Even being young, I remember feeling cared for and loved by our wonderful neighbor, Mrs. Marble. That kindness has never been lost on me. To this day, it is still the best soup I've ever had, not just because it tasted delicious but because of the heart behind it. Every time I think of that, it encourages me to take food across the street or down the road to someone who may desperately need a hand, but will never ask for it."

—Abbye in Guthrie, OK

"When we were in seminary, money was tight and we were far from home. We realized all the newly married couples living in our apartments were in the same situation and no one was really able to go home for Thanksgiving. I told my husband I wanted to host Thanksgiving dinner and invite everyone. He was so sweet to agree. We sent out invitations and twenty or twenty-five people came for dinner! It was important to me everyone had a place to sit, but our apartment was the smallest of small. So we moved out all of our living room furniture, borrowed folding tables and chairs from a church, and set up our living room like a cafeteria! To serve the food buffet-style, we had to walk around our apartment building and come in the back door to make our plates! It was so much fun we hosted four years straight, and it grew in number because everybody was having babies! I made turkey, mac and cheese, dressing, broccoli salad, collards, pumpkin pie, and rolls. These are the southern meals I grew up on but were new to some of our neighbors. The sweetest memories!"

—Lindsey in Ozark, MO

"My grandfather passed away on Father's Day in 2012. We were gathered at the family farm taking our turns having a last moment with him. In their small town of just over two thousand people, the news had traveled fast, and it wasn't long before there was a knock on the door. It was a neighbor dropping off a warm dish of food with other fixings piled on top, wrapped in foil. Opening the dish, my sister and I quickly realized this sweet lady, upon hearing the news of our grandfather's passing, must've literally wrapped up the Father's Day meal she had been preparing for her family. I think of this act often. Actually, nearly every time since 2012 that I've cooked a large meal, at some point in the stressful, time-consuming process, I think of the selflessness she showed our family that day—how the best part of going through the arduous process of cooking a holiday meal is to serve it to the people you love! Instead, she scooped up her hard work and gave it to another family at the last minute."

—Meredith in Bentonville, AR

"My husband and I run a small nonprofit organization that focuses on children's and widows' ministry here in the US and in Nigeria. We spend at least

163

one month a year in Nigeria spreading the love and hope of Jesus. The women that we minister to are in dire conditions and most times have no idea how they are going to feed their families. When we go, we take fifty-pound bags of rice, beans, flour, salt, and other staples that will hopefully last them at least a couple of months. They don't speak much English and my husband only speaks a small bit of their dialect. He gives a message and it is translated so they understand. At the end, when they are given bags to collect the food we brought for them, they literally weep with joy. They get on their knees and thank Jesus for providing food for their families. You see, they may not speak the same language as us, but food and hospitality are worldwide love languages. They know that through Jesus their prayers are answered, and for that they are forever grateful. By showing these women we care, by bringing them food to help them provide for their families, we are showing the love and hope of Jesus, being His hands and feet. Food is such a simple thing, but it literally changes lives and situations, and I know that is exactly what Jesus wants."

—Kandis in Belamawr, NJ

"One year I sent out an email to my family and friends. The email had a list of favorites for them to fill out. I had them list their favorite meal, dessert, candy, ice cream, cake, cookie, author, color, music, soft drink, fast food, Starbucks order, restaurant, perfume, flower, and hobby. They emailed me back all of their answers. I actually made the lists into a small scrapbook so I could reference it quickly when they had a bad day, or a family member was sick, or even for their birthday. This way I would have a list of things I could get quickly that I knew they would like."

—Cathy in Mountain Home, AR

"As a Lay Eucharist Minister, I take Communion to those that are unable to go to church. It is mostly elderly people who are living in assisted living facilities, nursing homes, or sometimes in their homes. They miss receiving Communion and the fellowship of being at church. I say a small service, followed by prayers and Scripture reading together. They thank me for remembering them, for being with them, and for caring enough to take the time after church to bring them Communion. It is so rewarding to help these souls as they journey toward the end of their lives. It is such a heartwarming and holy experience to minister to those in need and to the forgotten."

—Molly in Sunshine, LA

"My daddy passed on a cold December morning. We had been by his bed at the hospital for ten days. We were brokenhearted, and if I am being honest, exhausted. The morning following his death, I heard someone knocking at Mama's back door. It was seven o'clock in the morning and bitter cold. There stood Bettie B. Freeman with a platter of hot sausage biscuits—homemade biscuits nonetheless! I will never forget her or that morning."

—Maxine in Wilmington, NC

"When our first child was born, we were twenty and had only been married for seven months. Money was extremely tight, and we were living on ramen noodles and hot dogs multiple times a week. Our church lined up meals for us for a week or so, and I'll never forget a lady I hardly knew came by one evening with Jack Stack BBQ, a beloved Kansas City restaurant. The meal she delivered probably equaled our grocery budget for a week or two, and it meant so much to me that practically a stranger would bring us such a wonderful meal that we wouldn't be able to even dream of affording for several years. Almost twenty-one years later I still haven't forgotten her kindness; and when signing up to take a meal to a young family, I try to think of things to include that are extra little splurges that hopefully they'll enjoy."

—Amy in Harrisonville, MO

"We had internationally adopted three children when I became very ill. Doctors couldn't pin down the issue. I went often to appointments, and everyone was frustrated that I was so mysteriously sick. I was lethargic, swollen, and had bad blood counts. I even had a bone marrow tap scheduled. One day I had terrible pain and went to the emergency room, where I waited for three hours. Upon being seen, I was told that I was pregnant and dilated to an eight! It turned out that I had been preeclamptic, and that's why I had been so sick! My family and friends called each other, met up, and while I was laboring, they made lists of what would be needed. All of my previously adopted kids had come home at older ages, so I had nothing at home for a baby under the age of one. When I got home three days later with a new baby, all of my kids had been well cared for in my absence, and my friends and family had come into my home, completely setting it up for a newborn's arrival! It was pure magical love of those friends that carried me through for months, including kid-friendly meals and listening ears as I processed the events and the new chaos of my life!"

—Meri in Joplin, MO

"I worked at a Baptist college, and each week on Thursday night a group of missionary kids (MK) would show up for dinner around my table. Because their families were serving all over the world, I had their parents send me their MK's favorite recipe. I taught myself to make dishes from all over the world. One night an MK from Central Asia walked into my house in Mississippi and said, 'Oh, Aunt

Phala! It smells like home.' She lifted the lid on the pot and said, 'It also looks like home!' Some weeks the kids would come early to my house, take over my kitchen, and cook something they loved from their overseas home country, and we shared it around my table. Each of those MKs was a huge blessing in my life!"

—Phala in Sugar Hill, GA

"When I think of hospitality and love, welcome, serve, the first place my mind goes is to the summer and fall of 2016. I was put on bed rest at twenty-one weeks pregnant with our now five-year-old twin boys. My husband farms, and June is one of the busiest months of the year for the farm as they are harvesting wheat and working twelve-hour-plus days, often six to seven days a week. When we found out that I needed to be resting in bed (other than getting out for doctors' appointments or a quick shower or trip to the restroom), my first thought was, *He is going to have to live on frozen pizza rolls or fast food for weeks!* This is where our community showed up in a big way. Once word got out that I was on bed rest, family, friends, and church members jumped into action. They coordinated the bringing of meals and would often complete small household tasks like emptying the dishwasher or getting our mail when they brought food to drop off. The small gesture of a simple meal was so appreciated! When our boys came at twenty-six weeks and five days in July, we found ourselves two hours from home for four months while they got stronger in the NICU. Our community continued to show up, bringing us takeout meals when they visited! Or they would simply send gift cards to nearby restaurants or food delivery services. When it was finally time to bring the boys home, we came home to a fridge stocked with groceries and a freezer full of meals for us to easily heat, as we were in a sleep-deprived fog and learning to navigate life with twin babies. Bed rest and a long-term hospital stay often made me feel so lonely, but just the simple act of someone offering to bring a meal or texting us a gift card made me feel so loved and cared for during the hardest time in my life. I'm often asked now,

What should people do to love on families in the NICU?, and I always suggest feeding them. It feeds them both physically and spiritually to be loved on and remembered through food and hospitality."

—Erin in Iron City, TN

"I grew up with a mom who was the queen of hospitality, and we had folks for meals regularly. I don't really know why, but the thought of hosting always has created a lot of anxiety for me. Oh, I have done it many times over the years, but always with the blanket of anxiety. But with a heart that still desired to demonstrate hospitality, I decided that I could love friends, neighbors, and strangers by taking hospitality to them! I purchased four large square baskets that perfectly hold a full meal plus flowers or some little gift. The baskets allow me to be ready to deliver hospitality—they just have to return the basket or leave it on the porch for pickup. Whether it be an impromptu meal for a busy working mama, a new-baby meal, new-neighbor cookies, or food for a funeral, I have a basket ready to go. And now I have become more comfortable hosting in my home because the baskets have given me confidence, showing hospitality on terms that fit my personality."

—Jeanie in Wichita, KS

"Almost four years ago, within a span of about three months, my youngest child was diagnosed with a rare genetic syndrome and my dad was diagnosed with a terminal brain tumor. While my dad was rapidly declining, my daughter was having numerous tests and appointments. I was doing everything I could to be a wife, a mom of six, and a daughter, but I was completely overwhelmed. A friend showed up on my front porch one afternoon with two plastic bins filled with muffins and pastries and granola bars and Goldfish crackers. She told me that when I didn't have the capacity to come up with breakfast or a snack for one of my kiddos to send them to the bucket. It was the biggest blessing to me and to my family. Fast forward to this fall, and I was able to do the same thing for a family in our church who unexpectedly lost their wife and mom to COVID. The snack buckets were such a simple idea, but they made such a huge impact on my heart and in my life."

—Rebekah in Fayetteville, AR

"My husband is a high school football coach, and for years every Friday after school, we fed a dozen or so boys on our back porch before games. It wasn't fancy, but I believe that seeds of heaven were in those meals and in our fellowship on the back porch. We see the fruit as those boys are now getting married and having families of their own. Set an open table, and God shows up every time. Even in the midst of hungry high school football players!"

—Stephanie in Waynesville, OH

"In January 2013, my life changed forever. My dad, who was seventy-eight years old, decided to cut down a tree in his yard. I happened to be at my parents' home when this occurred. The tree fell onto him, breaking both large bones in both of his legs. He was hospitalized for five weeks and then sent to a local nursing home for rehab. Unfortunately, he became depressed after three weeks in rehab, so I helped my mom make the necessary arrangements to bring him back home to their house. The morning we were to sign him out of rehab, my mom suffered a fatal heart attack in their den at home. She was my heart, my best friend, and the glue of our family. I prayed so hard that day for the Lord to not just walk beside me but to carry me through that horrible time. After the funeral, I brought Dad back to his house. I was mentally and physically exhausted. The weeks that followed Mom's funeral were the toughest I have ever experienced. I wondered how I was going to be able to manage twelve-hour shifts taking care of my dad and still be a good wife and stepmother to our college-aged son who lived with us at the time. Well, God showed up and showed out for me. For the next eight weeks, I had meals provided every single day. On weekends, people even provided breakfast! What a blessing to be able to carry meals to my dad's and also have a hot meal with my husband and son each evening. The ones who brought meals were not only our friends, but also people I'd never met until they knocked on our door with food. I made so many new Christian friends from this outpouring of Christ's love for me! I received countless prayers offered by strangers-turned-friends while standing in my kitchen. I will never be able to thank God enough for showing me how He loves us through food and friends new and old."

—Lynn in North Augusta, SC

♥ ♥ ♥

"My dearest friend, Elizabeth, has taught me so much about generosity. For twenty-plus years, she has blessed friends new and old and has connected with probably hundreds through what I call her 'chicken soup ministry.' She makes and keeps on hand homemade, savory chicken broth and adds all the yummies, including noodles or rice, when she delivers. It might be shared with someone sick or recovering, maybe to someone who just needs encouragement. Sometimes she shares with someone she just met. I've also been the lucky recipient of her soul-warming and healing soup! She always makes folks feel seen and cared for. She truly is the hands and feet of Jesus! What an example of hospitality with a warm bowl of soup."

—Shari in Colorado Springs, CO

♥ ♥ ♥

"I'm writing in honor of my husband, Mark, who moved to heaven on Christmas Day 2020 after complications from the flu. Mark and I met in college, married in 1989, and built an amazing family of five children. Throughout our thirty-five years together I watched my husband become Mr. Hospitality. He loved people! He loved being surrounded by lots of people. He loved hosting and feeding people. In our early married life, it started as hosting friends for dinner and a yearly holiday party. He always loved hosting family holiday events. And by family, I mean any human who wanted to come to our home!

As our family grew, our children always knew they could invite anyone over, and Dad would always feed them. We had a pool, and our home became the team-party, cast-party, Sunday-evening neighbor dinner spot. The more people Mark could cook for, the better. Our home also became the place for belonging. Our kids always knew their friends were welcome. My husband never knew a stranger. When Mark moved to heaven, I was overwhelmed by the people who shared their thoughts about him with us. Mark was known for his cooking, welcoming spirit, bear hugs, amazing smile, and overwhelming love. He taught us all to use whatever gifts God has given us to love others."

—Aimee in Farmland, IN

"I took homemade granola and banana bread to my neighbors' doors during COVID and had sidewalk conversations with them to love them during a season of isolation."

—Angela in Huntsville, AL

"My son's baseball teammate passed away in a car accident in June. This friend had just graduated high school and was headed to college in the coming fall to play ball. Our boys had played baseball together since fourth grade, so we were close with this amazing young man and his mom. She's a single mom, and he was her only child—her world. One day, the Lord prompted me to make her a meal. She had just finished her first few weeks of teaching, and I knew it had been a rough week. I didn't want to give her a gift card because I wanted to make her something that would require very little effort for her. I prayed over her while I spent the afternoon preparing that meal of potato soup, salad, and chocolate chip cookies. And when I showed up on her doorstep, I was blessed by two hours of conversation, reminiscing, and lots of hugs and tears. We found ourselves both blessed and comforted. Sometimes I think the Lord blesses our hearts as much as the people we were hoping to bless."

—Lindsey in Lees Summit, MO

"In 2011 we moved our family out of a neighborhood and into the country. This was a difficult transition in many ways, one being that since we lived on acreage, we did not really see our neighbors in order to meet them. Well, that first Christmas season, my husband decided we would bake cookies and go caroling in order to meet them. Our kids were young teens at the time and were terrified of being humiliated! But that's what parents of teens do, right? Ha! So off we went, into the cold, dark December night with plates of cookies and trembling teens. We had a lot of fun meeting our neighbors and singing a carol on each porch. Fast forward a decade . . . our now-adult children ask when we are going caroling because they love the tradition! We also have sweet widowed neighbors who tell us each time how much they had been looking forward to our little visit and hoped we hadn't forgotten them. Such little things can be big things to the person on the receiving end of the kindness, but it can be so impactful and even life-changing for the giver."

—Leslie in Fayetteville, AR

"My husband was taken by ambulance to the ER after passing out. He had a dissected aorta and needed emergency heart surgery. Our twins were in sixth grade at the time, and the thought of losing my husband and their father was so overwhelming. In the days and weeks to come, we were ministered to by our church family in such ways that it truly was unbelievable. Every single day there was someone at our door with a meal. Some meals were elaborate and some very simple. It didn't matter. Words can't describe how we felt cared for with the thought that someone took the time and effort to cook for us. There is something about that gesture that shows the love of Jesus—and you never, ever forget it. To this day, some twenty years later, I can still remember the love that was shown to us, and it has influenced me to want to do for others what was done for my family. Truly, it doesn't need to be a fancy meal. Some of our favorites were just basic casseroles! I think that feeding people in their time of need is one of the best things you can do to show the love of Christ."

—Debbie in Ballwin, MO

"When my children were young, back in the '90s, we lived in a cul-de-sac. There were several families with children of similar ages. God led me to begin what the neighborhood came to call 'snack day.' Every Friday after school, I would set up a cheap plastic patio table in the front yard with some drinks and snacks. The snack ranged in simplicity from popcorn to barbecue beef sliders. But the food wasn't what mattered. The dozen or so neighborhood kids would be eagerly waiting for me to set up on the sidewalk in front of our house. After they snacked for a bit, they would turn their attention to playing in the cul-de-sac street. Kick the can, hide-and-seek, basketball, football, three flies up, etc., were favorites. The small act of placing something simple on a cheap table led to a neighborhood that became a sweetly knit-together community. Not only did the kids come out to play, but the parents came out of their houses too! Both moms and dads would bring their lawn chairs, and we would visit, console, celebrate, encourage, commiserate, and hold each other accountable. Many of us even ended up going to church together. Our neighborhood became a family.

We all look back on snack day with fond memories, not because of the food, but because of the love and welcome that came from the weekly gathering. One of the best outcomes of snack day is seeing echoes of it in my now-grown children. Now my daughter is a mom of three little ones who has embraced the Love Welcome Serve lifestyle, delivering meals to church members, friends, and neighbors who have a need. My son is a youth pastor for ages birth through high school and shares his love for group games, similar to those played on our street, with the kids at church. He is also known for some sort of food fun as he leads young minds to Jesus.

Looking back, I didn't have your words *love, welcome, serve,* but that was what snack day was all about. Through snack day our neighborhood made memories, ministered to each other, saw each other through many trials and victories, and were able to encourage each other in walking with Jesus through it all."

—Alison in Springdale, AR

"One of my favorite hospitality meal memories involves the precious widows of our congregation. One year, we decided to invite them to our home for a special Valentine's Day dinner. There is something sweet about a candlelit meal between two people in love, and we understood that they would likely be alone with no meal to look forward to on that day. We dressed up our humble dining room table with a pretty cloth and red roses. I made an Italian-themed dinner, and our children helped wait on the dear ones as we talked, laughed, and listened to details about their lives. It was a beautiful time to celebrate women who have loved and lost. When we planned the evening, our desire was to give them a night to enjoy, but the Lord once again demonstrated that it is truly better to give than to receive. Our family was blessed with their company. It is a Valentine's Day we will always treasure."

—Hillery in Nicholasville, KY

♥ ♥ ♥

"Two years ago my husband and I sat down to assess how we could be more intentional and love our neighbors in tangible ways. I began reading *The Gospel Comes with a House Key* by Rosaria Butterfield, and I realized that I do not need to possess some profound level of evangelism, nor do I need a perfect house. I am called to be the hands and feet of Jesus right where He has placed me. So I began to pray for our neighbors, asking God to provide opportunities for me to love and serve them.

That summer we picked way too many blueberries, and I knew exactly what to do with them—blueberry muffins! I had not met many neighbors yet, and I tend to be very introverted; so the idea of knocking on someone's door with food was quite a scary notion. I kept pushing off the idea because it seemed forward and weird. What if they didn't like them or even me? But I could not let go of the idea of baking these goodies and passing them out. The Holy Spirit continued to nudge me and press on my heart to reach out and be intentional. So I woke up one day and just did it, not allowing doubt to creep in. I had a specific neighbor I wanted to reach out to. Mrs. Becky usually comes outside midday to walk her dog. I kept looking out my window and never saw her. So I just prayed. I prayed that He'd keep me faithful to what was being pressed upon my heart, that He'd make me brave, and that she would come to the door. And when I courageously went outside, there she was walking outside too! She was so grateful to have received this first batch of muffins, and she shared sorrow with me from her past week, allowing me to pray with her.

The Enemy absolutely wants me to think that my introverted personality cannot be used by God. But I've now baked dozens of things for many neighbors. I leave notes on some, pray for many, and some neighbors have even turned into delightful friends. Baking breaks barriers!"

—Kaitlyn in Germantown, TN

"My husband has been a youth pastor for just over ten years. We have had the blessing of being at the same church (our first ministry) all those years. When we bought our house eight years ago, we knew we wanted to make a point to have an open-door policy when it came to having visitors. We wanted our home to be a place where people could come and go as they needed, hang out, and have fun.

My husband loves using his hands and building things, so he made us a beautiful farmhouse table using wood he got from his grandfather. The table was intentionally made bigger than our family of four needed so we could have the joy of sharing it with others. Each time a person comes over to share a meal or visit, we give them a Sharpie so they can sign the bottom of our table! Some think it's silly, but to us it's an incredible reminder of not only our ministry but also those lives we've been able to be a part of.

In our ten years of ministry, we have had many parents, grandparents, and students let us know how much of a difference we have made in the lives of many students. It's amazing to see how God can use something as simple as an open door to change the lives of others! We are making memories and leaving legacies around our table!"

—Alyssa in Paris, IL

"As I was leaving the gym one Saturday morning, I casually asked a friend how she was doing. Instead of the usual 'fine' or 'good' response I expected, she told me her week had been very hard. My first thought was that I would stop by the store on my way home and get some things to make a meal for her family. As we talked and she shared more about her situation, I remembered that I had a small casserole and a small pan of cinnamon rolls in the freezer. It would be perfect for their young family. When I asked her to stop by my house because I had something to give her, she agreed. Did I want to make a hot meal for her family? Of course! But when she came to pick up the food it didn't matter that it was still frozen and in the foil pans straight from the freezer. What mattered was that she felt loved, and I was given the opportunity to be the hands and feet of Christ."

—Cheryl in Ada, OK

♥ ♥ ♥

"In 1997, my family and I were living in St. Joseph, Missouri. I was struggling with ongoing postpartum depression, and the simplest of tasks seemed overwhelming. Prior to my depression, I had loved to cook and bake. I grew up on a Nebraska farm where we raised our own meat and produce and we made everything from scratch. We even had family cookbooks in print. Yet depression seemed to steal all that away, and even following a simple recipe became difficult.

On one particularly challenging day, I went to the grocery store to buy some basic items like deli meat, cheese, bread, milk, etc. I noticed a young mom and a baby wandering around the store looking a bit lost and alone. We made eye contact, and she made her way over to my cart. We greeted each other, and I asked her a simple question: 'What can I do for you today?' She responded by telling me that she and her husband were missionaries who traveled on foot, and they had run out of food.

Overcoming my curiosity about the truthfulness of their story, I put them in my car and took them to my home. I phoned my husband at work to come home as soon as possible, and I phoned a couple of friends to ask for their prayers as we welcomed complete strangers into our home. Our meal that night was simple: ham and cheese sandwiches, chips, fruit, and ice cream. We also paid for them to spend the night in a hotel, sending them off with snacks and basic items for their baby. When we said our goodbyes, I asked the young mom what was in the grocery store that made her trust me to help them. She answered with something like, 'You simply asked, What can I do for you today? Not tomorrow or the future, but today. We were hungry and you fed us today.' I realized then how important it is for us to follow God's promptings every day.

It would have been so easy for me to ignore her in the grocery store or just give her some money to make her go away. He showed me that He can use me even in my brokenness and depression. God fed us both on that day: physical food for this woman and her family and spiritual food for me."

—Renee in Wintzville, MO

"We moved to Georgia from the Midwest for my husband's job at a particular chicken restaurant known for their hospitality. In the Midwest we know how to whip up a good casserole or throw together a delicious coffee cake, but the South? The South knows its food. Here I was, an introvert, two kids under two, knowing no one, and I had no idea how to make a proper biscuit. So I began to learn.

Food became my creativity outlet. I would devour cookbooks, cooking shows, baking championships, whatever I could. Opening up our doors became a lifeline, a way to welcome and meet new people, to show them the love of Jesus. I'd pray for them as I'd stir the soup that would soon fill their bellies. We'd sit and listen to their stories of God's faithfulness. Our bodies would be nourished, and so would our souls. I never let a Meal Train go by without signing up. I'd drop cookies off on porches every Christmas. Hospitality became a way of life; we'd open our hearts to wherever the Spirit would lead. Sometimes we opened our doors and shared a meal, and sometimes I'd drop off some cookies on a friend's porch.

We've been in Georgia for six years now. I'm still an introvert. I now have three kids, and I'm happy to say I think I can make a proper biscuit! Most importantly, we have fed and welcomed hundreds of people into our lives and home to the glory of Jesus. Testimonies have been shared, many prayers have been prayed, and many memories have been made. I have learned that hospitality is a posture of the heart. I pray the Lord keeps my heart in the right place, knowing that I don't have to entertain, but rather inviting His presence to come. We will share in the ultimate meal at the wedding feast, on that beautiful day when our Beloved returns for us, but until then we will keep opening our hearts and our homes . . . all the more as we see the day approaching."

—Allison in Newnan, GA

from the author

*H*i, dear one! This is just an extra little from-me-to-you minute. I'm so glad you've spent this time with me in a biblical hospitality deep-dive. The fullness and satisfaction of being used so humbly by a great God in the lives of others through a life given to hospitality is hard to beat. I'm praying for you to make soup or grab takeout, extend an intentional invitation, and love people well! But I wanted to share a final thought—and this one is personal.

We've seen Jesus at the table with all kinds of different people, those who were near and those who were far from God. We've seen Him in various hospitality roles: guest, host, cook, and servant. We've witnessed Him offering invitations and accepting invitations to engage with people in spiritual things. But there is one final invitation that needs to be shared, and that is an invitation for you!

In Revelation 3:20, Jesus said, "Here I am! I stand at the door and knock. If anyone hears my voice and opens the door, I will come in and eat with that person, and they with me."

What a beautiful picture! Imagine it—Jesus standing at a door knocking because He desires to engage with *you* at the table. Like He did with Zacchaeus, with Mary and Martha, with Peter on the shore, Jesus Christ is initiating a hospitality encounter with you, knocking patiently at the door of your heart, extending an invitation to enjoy friendship and community with Him. He graciously beckons you to allow Him to come into your life and satisfy your soul. His desire is to know you and be known by you, to talk with you and be heard by you.

Consider the kind of relationship that Christ seeks with you: "I will come in and eat with that person, and they with me." Jesus used the imagery of gathering together around a shared meal, eating together, as the ultimate in intimate friendship. Friendly, warm, and personal. Feasting on His goodness. Satisfied by the Bread of Life who never leaves you longing for more.

What an invitation this is! Can you even imagine? Jesus Christ, the King of kings and Lord of lords wants to have a personal relationship with you! He invites you to come to Him and enjoy the abundance of a changed life around His table.

In Matthew 11:28, Jesus said, "Come to me, all you who are weary and burdened, and I will give you rest." Christ invites you to His table because He knows that life is heavy with difficulty, pain, isolation, and despair. A seat at His table offers peace and comfort, a respite from the harshness of life.

In John 10:10, Jesus said, "I have come that they may have life, and have it to the full." Christ invites you to His table because the fullest life is found in Him—a life of favor, a life of purpose, a life with meaning.

In John 6:35, Jesus said, "I am the bread of life. Whoever comes to me will never go hungry, and whoever believes in me will never be thirsty." Christ invites you to His table because He knows that nothing else the world offers will ever satisfy the hunger and thirst of your soul.

This is the hope of Jesus! Oh, how I hope you'll consider this greatest invitation ever extended!

Maybe you don't yet know Him, and you've never pursued a personal relationship with Jesus. Dear one, I encourage you to open the door to your heart and allow Him to come in. I know you're hungry for more than what this world has fed you thus far. Look to Him! Confess your sin and muck, your selfishness and pride, and run to Him in faith and belief. Ask Him to forgive you and to save you from yourself. And you'll find that a seat at His table will be yours for all eternity!

Even if you do know Him, He knocks at your door too. He invites you to dine with Him continually, to walk with Him and abide in Him each day. He seeks to commune with you intimately through His Word, His Spirit, and His church. Open the door of your heart, and be filled daily from your seat at His table!

Maybe you've found yourself having walked away from Him. Your relationship with Jesus may have been very real in the past, but things have gotten complicated. Friend, the world is hard. You're not alone. Heartbreak, betrayal, grief, or addiction may have thrown you a curveball and your spiritual life may have been derailed. Your church life may have become nonexistent. You've been distant from the Lord for too long, and you're aching inside, thirsty. Listen, your most gracious Father stands and knocks at your door as well. At the table, He has kept your seat warm, and He longs for your return.

Wherever you find yourself, the invitation is yours. Hear Him from the shore: "Friend, come and eat!"

notes

INTRODUCTION: THE ETERNAL SIGNIFICANCE OF EVERYDAY HOSPITALITY

1. Ruth Reichl, *My Kitchen Year: 136 Recipes That Saved My Life: A Cookbook* (New York: Random House, 2015), xvii.

CHAPTER 1: THE PRACTICE AND PURPOSE

1. Dr. Sam Hannon, personal conversation with author.
2. Amy Hannon, *Love Welcome Serve: Recipes That Gather and Give* (New York: Hachette Book Group, 2017).

CHAPTER 2: PEOPLE OVER PRESENTATION

1. Dictionary.com, s.v. accessed May 25, 2022, https://www.dictionary.com/browse/entertain.
2. Jeff Christopherson, "Jeff Christopherson on the Power of Biblical Hospitality," *Urban Christian News,* August 19, 2019, https://urbanchristiannews.com/2019/08/jeff-christopherson-on-the-power-of-biblical-hospitality.

CHAPTER 3: LOVE: THE MOTIVATION

1. Women of Welcome, (@womenofwelcome), Instagram photo, January 7, 2022, https://www.instagram.com/p/CYbsk5kNSYF/.

CHAPTER 4: WELCOME: THE INVITATION

1. *Merriam-Webster*, s.v. "welcome," accessed May 31, 2022, https://www.merriam-webster.com/dictionary/welcome; "the word derives from the Old English *wilcuma*, meaning "a desired/desirable guest," https://www.oxfordlearnersdictionaries.com/us/definition/english/welcome_2.

2. "Diving Deeper into Christ-Like Welcome," Christ-Like Welcome (blog), Women of Welcome, accessed May 31, 2022, https://womenofwelcome.com/christlikewelcome-blog.

3. Tara John, "How the World's First Loneliness Minister Will Tackle 'the Sad Reality of Modern Life,'" *TIME*, April 25, 2018, https://time.com/5248016/tracey-crouch-uk-loneliness-minister/.

4. Shauna Niequist, (@sniequist), Instagram photo, January 10, 2022, https://www.instagram.com/p/CYjWn26L_rT/.

5. Dustin Willis and Brandon Clements, *The Simplest Way to Change the World: Biblical Hospitality As a Way of Life* (Chicago: Moody, 2017), 20.

6. Ann Voskamp, quoted in Kristen deRoo VanderBerg, "Inspire: Living Lives of Abundant Hospitality," Christian Reformed Church in North America, August 6, 2019, https://www.crcna.org/news-and-events/news/inspire-living-lives-abundant-hospitality.

CHAPTER 5: SERVE: THE OPERATION

1. Lexico.com, s.v. "generous," accessed May 31, 2022, https://www.lexico.com/en/definition/generous.

2. Bob Goff, *Love Does: Discover a Secretly Incredible Life in an Ordinary World* (Nashville: Thomas Nelson, 2012), xvi.

CHAPTER 6: JESUS: THE MODEL

1. Tim Chester, *A Meal with Jesus: Discover Grace, Community, and Mission Around the Table* (Wheaton, IL: Crossway, 2011), 13.

2. Rosaria Butterfield, *The Gospel Comes with a House Key* (Crossway, 2018), https://vimeo.com/262120176.

CHAPTER 8: JESUS: THE MAGNIFIED

1. John Piper, "Glorifying God . . . Period," Campus Outreach Staff Conference, Orlando, FL, July 15, 2013, https://www.desiringgod.org/messages/glorifying-god-period.

GATHER & GIVE: A HOSPITALITY HANDBOOK

1. Jean Anthelme Brillat-Savarin, *The Physiology of Taste: Or Meditations on Transcendental Gastronomy (Vintage Classics)* (New York: Vintage, 2011), 16.
2. Shauna Niequist, *Bread and Wine: A Love Letter to Life Around the Table* (Grand Rapids: Zondervan, 2020), 270.
3. For complete recipes and menus for gathering and giving, grab a copy of my cookbook *Love Welcome Serve: Recipes That Gather and Give* (Nashville: Center Street, 2018) on ShopEunaMaes.com.

gratitude

$\mathcal{I}$t's rare that I ever sing songs of thankfulness without becoming a big, weepy puddle on the floor, so penning gratitude has a very similar effect on me. God has been so kind to surround me with the people that I love, a family who means the world to me, and opportunities that I would've never imagined in my wildest dreams. He wired me to crave relationships with people and to desire to put things into the world that inspire and delight. And by golly, that's the work I get to do every day by His grace. So above all, I'm grateful to the Lord Jesus for His abundant favor. All to Him I owe.

By this point, I have said Sam Hannon's name about 574 times, because he's my guy in ministry and life, my hospitality sidekick, my cheerleader, my sous chef, and my forever date. There are not enough words to accurately represent the level of help and support he gave me in writing this book. He has quite possibly pored over this manuscript more times than all the editors combined because I continually sought his insight, his knowledge, and his confirmation—all of which I value so much. What I'm saying is that I bugged him to death over every paragraph in this book. And he was a gem. Sam Hannon (that's 575 times), your encouragement, wisdom, and partnership in this project was a gift. *Gather & Give* wouldn't be the book it is without you.

Grace, Luke, Ally, and Isaac Hannon. Gosh, I love y'all more than you'll ever know. Out of all of the big, fun opportunities I've enjoyed, none of them give me the joy that you all do. Thanks for cheering for me and for always coming home. My heart and my door will forever be open to you.

My parents, Larry and Brenda Nelson, think I'm amazing. They do! I'm just being honest. They cheer for me and sing my praises to their friends, neighbors, church family, and strangers, I feel sure. They have always been so proud of who I am and what I do, which has given me all kinds of security and confidence to follow the Lord in this hospitality journey. Mom and Dad, thanks for your encouragement and for believing in me! Here's to impromptu tacos and Sunday lunches together for the rest of our days!

Speaking of believing in me, my literary agent takes the cake! Shannon Marven, you are so good to me. I continue to be genuinely humbled by your support and belief in me. Thank you for courting and pursuing me years ago! And thank you for your continual encouragement and hard work to make sure that this hospitality message makes it onto pages of books.

To my editor, Stephanie Newton, and the team at W Publishing: you all wow me with your experience and knowledge, your patience and help! It's a privilege to author under your leadership! You've been wonderful! Thank you for partnering with me on *Gather & Give*. Your expertise sure makes me look good! Grateful!

To my treasured, kindred Euna Mae's community: You keep showing up for me at gatherings, suppers, and events. In my retail store, in my social media feeds, and in auditoriums far and wide. Meeting you and moving quickly to common ground is one of my greatest delights! You are fun! You are joy! And you'll never know the depths of my gratitude for your friendship and faithfulness to me. I truly and humbly mean it with all my heart.

And finally, my hospitality heroes. Gosh, there have been countless people over the course of my life who have opened their doors, extended a welcome, demonstrated hospitality, and been Jesus to me. Women from First Baptist Church in Mountain Home, Arkansas, where I grew up. Mothers of high school and college friends, who shared grace and warmth in my life, who gave me a home away from home. Families at Fellowship Bible Church Northwest Arkansas, who have modeled Jesus and hospitality for me for almost thirty years. To each and every one of you: Your simple gestures of biblical hospitality left a significant spiritual mark on my heart. I am who I am because of your collective kindness and grace.

about the author

*A*my Nelson Hannon lives in Northwest Arkansas in the heart of the Ozark Mountains. She is married to her college sweetheart, Sam, who is the smartest and funniest boy in the world. Her three greatest gifts came packaged as Grace, Luke, and Isaac. Amy cut her hospitality teeth as a preacher's wife in the South where it's a way of life to share a meal for just about every reason on earth. She learned quickly what a joy it is to share good food and life around the table with friends and neighbors for God's glory.

Amy owns Euna Mae's, a one-of-a-kind kitchen boutique named after her grandmother. She authored a comfort food cookbook titled *Love Welcome Serve*, and she hosted her own cooking show for several years on Northwest Arkansas's NBC affiliate. Amy speaks to women, hosts curated travel excursions and table events, and drums up all kinds of experiences in order to share her simple, biblical hospitality message. Love deeply, welcome gladly, and serve faithfully so that in all things God may be praised (1 Peter 4:8–11).

Amy wishes she knew how to quilt, is a spirited sports fan, and can't help but bake an apple pie on the first crisp day of autumn.